THE
GOSPEL
FOR LIFE

—— SERIES ——

THE GOSPEL &

Racial
Reconciliation

THE
GOSPEL
FOR LIFE

—— SERIES ——

THE GOSPEL &

Racial
Reconciliation

SERIES EDITORS

RUSSELL MOORE *and*
ANDREW T. WALKER

B&H
PUBLISHING GROUP
NASHVILLE, TENNESSEE

978-1-4336-9046-4

Published by B&H Publishing Group
Nashville, Tennessee

Dewey Decimal Classification: 261.83
Subject Heading: GOSPEL \ RACE RELATIONS \
CHURCH AND RACE RELATIONS

1 2 3 4 5 6 7 8 • 21 20 19 18 17 16

CONTENTS

Series Preface

Russell Moore

Why Should *The Gospel for Life* Series Matter to Churches?

IN ACTS CHAPTER 2, WE READ ABOUT THE DAY OF PENTECOST, the day when the resurrected Lord Jesus sent the Holy Spirit. The Day of Pentecost was a spectacular day—there were manifestations of fire, languages being spoken by people who didn't know them, and thousands of unbelievers coming to faith in this recently resurrected Messiah. Reading this passage, we go from account to account of heavenly shock and awe, and yet the passage ends in an unexpectedly simple way: "And they devoted themselves to the apostles' teaching and the fellowship, to the breaking of bread and the prayers" (Acts 2:42).

I believe one thing the Holy Spirit wants us to understand from this is that these "ordinary" things are not less miraculous than what preceded them—in fact, they may be more so. The disciplines of discipleship, fellowship, community, and prayer are the signs that tell us the kingdom of Christ is here. That means that for Christians, the most crucial moments in our walk with Jesus Christ don't happen in the thrill of "spiritual highs." They happen in the common hum of everyday life in quiet, faithful obedience to Christ.

That's what *The Gospel for Life* series is about: taking the truths of Scripture, the story of our redemption and adoption by a risen Lord Jesus, and applying them to the questions and situations that we all face in the ordinary course of life.

Our hope is that churches will not merely find these books interesting, but also helpful. *The Gospel for Life* series is meant to assist pastors and church leaders to answer urgent questions that people are asking, questions that the church isn't always immediately ready to answer. Whether in a counseling session or alongside a sermon series, these books are intended to come alongside church leaders in discipling members to see their lives with a Kingdom mentality.

Believers don't live the Christian life in isolation but rather as part of a gospel community, the church. That's why we have structured *The Gospel for Life* series to be easily utilized in anything from a small group study context to a new member or new believer class. None of us can live worthy of the gospel by ourselves and, thankfully, none have to.

Why are we so preoccupied with the idea of living life by and through the gospel? The answer is actually quite simple: because the gospel changes everything. The gospel isn't a mere theological system or a political idea, though it shapes both our theology and our politics. The gospel is the Good News that there is a Kingdom far above and beyond the borders of this world, where death is dead and sin and sorrow cease. The gospel is about how God brings this Kingdom to us by reconciling us to Himself through Christ.

That means two things. First, it means the gospel fulfills the hopes that our idols have promised and betrayed. The Scripture says that all God's promises are yes in Jesus (2 Cor. 1:20). As sinful human beings, we all tend to think what we really want is freedom from authority, inheritance without obedience like the prodigal son. But what Jesus offers is the authority we were designed to live under, an inheritance we by no means deserve to share, and the freedom that truly satisfies our souls.

Second, this means that the gospel isn't just the start of the Christian life but rather the vehicle that carries it along. The gospel is about the daily reality of living as an adopted child of a resurrected Father-King, whose Kingdom is here and is still coming. By looking at our jobs, our marriages, our families, our government, and the entire universe through a gospel lens, we live differently. We will work and marry and vote with a Kingdom mind-set, one that prioritizes the permanent things of

Christ above the fleeting pleasures of sin and the vaporous things of this world.

The Gospel for Life series is about helping Christians and churches navigate life in the Kingdom while we wait for the return of its King and its ultimate consummation. The stakes are high. To get the gospel wrong when it comes to marriage can lead to a generation's worth of confusion about what marriage even is. To get the gospel wrong on adoption can leave millions of "unwanted" children at the mercy of ruthless sex traffickers and callous abusers. There's no safe space in the universe where getting the gospel wrong will be merely an academic blunder. That's why these books exist—to help you and your church understand what the gospel is and what it means for life.

Theology doesn't just think; it walks, weeps, and bleeds. *The Gospel for Life* series is a resource intended to help Christians see their theology do just that. When you see all of life from the perspective of the Kingdom, everything changes. It's not just about miraculous moments or intense religious experiences. Our gospel is indeed miraculous, but as the disciples in Acts learned, it's also a gospel of the ordinary.

Introduction

Andrew T. Walker

RACIAL RECONCILIATION REPRESENTS ONE OF THE MOST volatile issues in contemporary America. Recent events—whether in Ferguson, Missouri, or Charleston, South Carolina—remind us that America's wounds on race are still deep. But we cannot allow our failures as a society to simply simmer. In every age, the prophetic imagination must be engaged in hopes of making progress. We saw this in Martin Luther King Jr.'s day; and we must, and we are, seeing it in our own.

To whom else can society look than the church to seek understanding where misunderstanding abounds?

The church must be on the frontier of racial reconciliation in America. In recent American past, it was the church that was one of the greatest impediments to racial justice in America; but it was also the church that helped inspire America and Americans to, to quote Dr. King, "cash this check, a check that will give us upon demand the riches of freedom and the security of justice."

To care about racial justice and racial reconciliation is to tap into the very best of the Christian story. Ours is a story that tells of a God who makes every one of His children precious in His sight. It is a story about a God who stamps His image on every person—regardless of color or ethnicity.

But to care about racial reconciliation as Christians isn't just about seeing the value of each person as an image bearer, as invaluable as that is; it's about picturing the reconciliation offered to each one of us in Christ. Apart from Christ, we were separated from God. Apart from Christ, humanity separates itself from one another. The wide lens of reconciliation between God and man also grants the reconciliation between the broken chains of humanity. In Christ, we no longer define ourselves by the color of our skin, but by shade of red blood that our Savior spilled to reconcile us.

Each book in *The Gospel for Life* series is structured the same: What are we for? What does the gospel say? How should the Christian live? How should the church engage? What does the culture say?

The Gospel & Racial Reconciliation is structured in such a way as to inform every angle of the Christian's life—their place in culture, their engagement as everyday Christians, and their role in the body of Christ, the church. We want no stone unturned when talking about how the gospel of Jesus Christ shapes us as a people on mission for God.

To that end, this book includes scholars and speakers, pastors and practitioners to address important issues related to racial reconciliation. *The Gospel & Racial Reconciliation* tackles all the subjects that a Christian would need to know to intelligently engage the topic at hand. In this volume, readers will learn about what the Bible says on race. Readers will see in practical detail how the gospel shapes our understanding of racial reconciliation. Finally, you'll receive practical insights as to what you might do in everyday life to engage this aspect of living as neighbors in diverse communities.

Racial reconciliation is a sensitive subject with which well-meaning people feel intimidated to engage. It seems, at times, there are too many landmines, and too many unforgiveable sins in the discourse. But in order for us to grow together, we must not let the headwinds of complexity discourage a steady course toward reconciliation. We hope Christians and their churches will be different after reading this book. We hope readers go from passive spectators to gospel change agents.

Personally, I have learned so much from contributors to this book amidst recent events that demonstrated America's ongoing racial tension. There are individuals, like myself, who learned to extend a sympathetic ear to narratives that can so easily be ignored. It was important for me to put my guard down; to set aside any prejudgments. That's just one small step, but an important one. In the same way, what readers take away from this book will be up to them. We hope one product of this shared experience will be discovery of a forgotten practice: listening.

Christians must see it as their individual and collective responsibility to be the change they're hoping to see. Who else can do this than the church?

CHAPTER

1

What Are We For?

J. Daniel Hays

IN A CULTURE FULL OF CONFLICTS, THINKING INSIDE (AND outside) the church can be reduced to an "us" against "them" mentality. We become defined, not only by our race, but by something or someone we are against.

But what if, rather than being known for what we are *against*, Christians defined our identity, and the identities, therefore, of our neighbors, by what we are *for*?

We Are for the Image of God

First, we are those who are *for* the dignity of image of God in every person. Any serious biblical study of race or ethnicity should start in Genesis 1. The Bible does not start off with the creation of a special or privileged race of people. When the first human being is created he is simply called *adam*, which is Hebrew for "humankind." Adam and Eve are not Hebrews or Egyptians; they are neither white nor black nor even Semitic. Their own particular ethnicity is not even mentioned, for the Bible seems to stress that they are the mother and father of all peoples of all ethnicities. Adam and Eve are presented as non-ethnic and non-national because they represent all people of all ethnicities.

In Genesis 1:26 God says, "Let us make man [*adam*] in our image, after our likeness." Then 1:27 describes His creative action: "So God created man [*adam*] in his own image; He created him in the image of God; He created them male and female." The "image of God" relates to one or more of the following: 1) the mental and spiritual faculties that people share with God; 2) the appointment of humankind as God's representatives on earth; and 3) a capacity to relate to God. Yet what is clear is that being created in "the image of God" is a spectacular blessing; it is what distinguishes people from animals. Likewise, whether or not the "image of God" in people was marred or blurred in the Fall of Genesis 3, it is clear that at the very least people still carry some aspect of the image of God, and this gives humankind a very special status in the creation. Furthermore, as mentioned above, Adam and Eve are ethnically generic, representing all ethnicities.

Thus the Bible is very clear in declaring from the beginning that all people of all races and ethnicities carry the image of God.

This reality provides a strong starting point for our discussion of what the Bible says about race. Indeed, John Stott declares, "Both the dignity and the equality of human beings are traced in Scripture to our creation."[1] To presuppose that one's own race or ethnicity is superior to someone else's is a denial of the fact that *all people* are created in the image of God.

The book of Proverbs presents several practical implications from this connection between God and the people He created. For example, Proverbs 14:31 states, "The one who oppresses the poor insults his Maker" (HCSB). Proverbs 17:5 echoes this teaching, "The one who mocks the poor insults his Maker" (HCSB). These verses teach that those who take a superior attitude toward others due to their socioeconomic position and thus oppress or mock others are, in fact, insulting God Himself. To insult or mistreat the people God has created is an affront to Him, their Creator. The same principle applies to racial prejudice. The unjustified self-establishment of superiority by one group that leads to the oppression of other groups is an affront to God. Likewise, the mocking of people God created—and this would apply directly to ethnic belittling or "racial jokes"—is a direct insult to God. All people of all ethnicities are created in the image of God. Viewing them as such and, therefore, treating them with dignity and respect is not just a suggestion or "good manners," it is one of the mandates emerging out of Genesis 1 and Proverbs.

We Are Against Degrading God's Image (The So-Called "Curse of Ham," Genesis 9:18–27)

In regard to the history of racial prejudice in America, no other passage in Scripture has been as abused, distorted, and twisted as has Genesis 9:18–27. Thus it is important that we clarify what this passage actually says (and doesn't say).

In Genesis 9:20–21, after the flood is over and his family has settled down, Noah gets drunk and passes out, lying naked in his tent. His son Ham, specifically identified as the father of Canaan (9:22), sees him and tells his two brothers Shem and Japheth, who then carefully cover up their father. When Noah wakes up and finds out what happened he pronounces a curse on Canaan, the son of Ham, stating, "Cursed be Canaan! The lowest of slaves will he be to his brothers." Noah then blesses Shem and Japheth, declaring, "Blessed be the LORD, the God of Shem! May Canaan be the slave of Shem. May God extend the territory of Japheth . . . and may Canaan be his slave" (9:26–27 NIV).

In the nineteenth century, both before and after the Civil War, this text was frequently cited by whites to argue that the slavery or subjugation of the black races was, in fact, a fulfillment of the prophecy in this text. These pastors and writers argued that 1) the word *Ham* really means "black" or "burnt," and thus refers to the black race; and 2) God commanded that the descendants of Ham (black people) become slaves to Japheth, who, they argued, represents the white races.[2]

It should be stated clearly and unambiguously that every reputable evangelical Old Testament scholar that I know of views this understanding of Genesis 9:18–27 as ridiculous, even ludicrous. It is completely indefensible on biblical grounds.

First of all, note that the curse is placed on Canaan and not on Ham (Gen. 9:25). To project the curse to all of Ham's descendants is to misread the passage. It is Canaan (and the Canaanites) who are the focus of this curse. This text is a prophetic curse on Israel's future enemy and nemesis, the Canaanites. The Canaanites are included here in this prophetic curse because they are characterized by similar sexual-related sins elsewhere in the Pentateuch (see Lev. 18:2–23 for example). The curse on Canaan is not pronounced because Canaan is going to be punished for Ham's sin, but because the descendants of Canaan (the Canaanites) will be like Ham in their sin and sexual misconduct.

Furthermore, it is wildly speculative to assume that the name Ham actually means "black" and thus refers to the people in black Africa. There is an ancient Egyptian word *keme* that means "the black land," a reference to the land of Egypt and to the dark fertile soil associated with Egypt. Yet to assume that the Hebrew name Ham is even connected at all to this Egyptian word is questionable. Then even if it is, to say that "the black land," a reference to fertile soil, is actually a reference to black races in Africa is likewise quite a leap in logic. Thus the etymological argument that "Ham" refers to the black peoples of Africa is not defensible. Likewise, as mentioned above, the actual curse is on Canaan, who is clearly identified as the son of Ham. Thus the curse is placed on the Canaanites and not on the supposed (and unlikely) descendants of Ham in black Africa.

This passage finds fulfillment later in Israel's history during the conquest of the Promised Land when the Israelites defeat and subjugate the Canaanites. It has absolutely nothing to do with black Africa or the subjugation of black peoples. Such an interpretation seriously distorts and twists the meaning of this passage.

What Was the Ethnic Composition of Biblical Israel?

Using cultural and geographical "boundary markers" such as language, territory, religion, dress, appearance, and ancestor origins, the ancient peoples in the regions in and around ancient Israel can be split up into four major ethnic groups:

1. the Asiatics or Semites (including the Israelites, Canaanites, Amorites, Arameans, etc.);

2. the Cushites (black Africans living along the Nile River south of Egypt; also referred to as Nubians or Ethiopians, although they are not connected to modern Ethiopia);
3. the Egyptians (a mix of Asiatic, north African, and African elements); and
4. Indo-Europeans (Hittites, Philistines).

Ancient Israel develops from within the Asiatic/Semitic group of peoples, although several of the other groups have significant input. Note that Israel is not mentioned in Genesis 10 as one of the ancient peoples. When God first calls Abraham, he is living in Ur of the Chaldees, an Amorite region of Mesopotamia. Yet later in the Bible, Abraham is most closely associated with the Arameans (Gen. 24:4; 28:5; Deut. 26:5). While both Abraham's son Isaac and grandson Jacob marry Aramean women, the next generation also marries Canaanites (Judah, Gen. 38:2; Simeon, Gen. 46:10) and Egyptians (Joseph, Gen. 41:50).

Thus at the dawning of the Israelite nation, the descendants of Abraham are a mix of Western Mesopotamian (Aramean and/or Amorite), Canaanite, and Egyptian elements, and looked very much like the Semitic peoples of the Middle East today, such as modern Arabs and Israelis.

It is during the four-hundred-plus-year sojourn in Egypt that the family of Abraham develops linguistically and culturally into an identifiable Israelite people. Yet even then, in terms of ethnicity, they are hardly monolithic. In addition to the various ethnic streams that influence the formation of the Israelite nation during the patriarchal period, numerous other ethnic influences continued to shape the formation of Israel. For example, when God delivers Israel from Egypt, the Bible mentions that "an ethnically diverse crowd went up with them" (Exod. 12:38). This term indicates that the group Moses leads out of Egypt and into covenant relationship with God is an ethnically diverse group. The majority of them are probably descendants of Abraham but many of them are not.

At this particular time in Egypt's history, there are numerous Cushites (black Africans) living in Egypt, at all levels of society. In all likelihood some of these Africans are part of the "ethnically diverse crowd" that comes out of Egypt and joins Israel. During the Exodus, Moses will marry one of these Cushites (see below). Likewise, the name of Moses' great nephew Phinehas, a very prominent priest, suggests a connection with the Cushites. Phinehas's name is an Egyptian name. The Egyptians referred to the black African inhabitants of Cush by the ethnic term *nehsiu*. In Egyptian the prefix "ph" functions like a definite article, so the name "Phinehas" literally means "the Cushite" or "the African," that is, one of the black Africans living in Cush.

What about Moses and Interethnic Marriage?

In the books of Exodus, Leviticus, Numbers, and Deuteronomy, the central character, apart from God, is Moses. Appointed by God as Israel's leader and mediator between God and the people, Moses dominates the human side of the story. Interestingly, the biblical story includes quite a bit of personal information about Moses, even specifically mentioning his two interethnic marriages. Keep in mind that at this time in Israel's history the norm of monogamous marriage had not yet been established. Recall that even later in history King David will have seven wives, apparently with God's approval.

Early in Moses' life he flees from Egypt to Midian, where he meets and marries Zipporah, a Midian woman (Exod. 2). The Midianites are a Semitic-speaking people, ethnic cousins to the Israelites. What is surprising about this marriage is that the Midianites worship Baal. In fact, Reuel, Zipporah's father, is a priest of Midian (Exod. 2:15–22; Num. 25). At this stage of his life Moses is not serving God yet, and there is no indication that God approves of this marriage. Indeed, later in Numbers 25 the Midianites will appear as a deadly and dangerous theological enemy of Israel who threaten to undermine the theological and ethical faithfulness of Israel to God.

Later in his life, however, while Moses is faithfully leading Israel and serving God, he marries a Cushite woman (Num. 12:1).

In the past, some scholars, perhaps bothered by Moses' marriage to a black African woman, tried to argue that this woman is actually Zipporah the Midianite. Such an argument is quite weak, however. The Cushites are well-known in the Old Testament and there is nothing ambiguous about their identity or their ethnicity. Moses marries a black African woman; there is no doubt about this.[3]

Yet what of the biblical injunctions against interethnic marriage? Is Moses violating these commandments? Not at all. In the Pentateuch the prohibition against intermarrying with other groups always specifically refers to the pagan inhabitants of Canaan (Deut. 7:1–4). The reason for this prohibition is theological. If they intermarry with these pagan peoples, God warns, "They will turn your sons away from Me to worship other gods" (Deut. 7:4 HCSB; see also Exod. 34:15–16). Underscoring this distinction is Deuteronomy 21:10–14, which describes the procedure for how the Israelites *are to marry foreign women*, a practice that was allowed if the women are from cities that are outside that land; that is, not Canaanite. Later in Israel's history, Ezra and Nehemiah will reissue the prohibition against intermarriage (Ezra 9:1; Neh. 13:23–27), but once again the context is that of marrying outside the faith. Both Ezra and Nehemiah seem to stress that earlier intermarriages (especially Solomon's) played a negative role in Israel's apostasy and idolatry.

The implications of Moses' marriage to a Cushite woman are significant. Moses is one of the leading figures in the Old Testament. As the story unfolds in Numbers 12:1–16, it is clear that God approves of this marriage, for He rebukes Miriam and Aaron for opposing it, and He then strongly reaffirms Moses as His chosen leader. Thus early in Israel's story we find one of Israel's most faithful leaders intermarrying with a black African woman while serving God faithfully.

The conclusion we can draw from these Scripture passages is that interracial marriage is strongly affirmed by Scripture, if the marriage is within the faith. Marriage outside of the faith, however, is prohibited.

Which Ethnicities Play Central Roles in the Old Testament Story?

Ebed-Melech the Cushite plays a key role in the book of Jeremiah, both historically and theologically. Jeremiah the prophet preaches for years against the sinful actions of the leaders and the people in Judah, but meets only with rejection and hostility. As Jeremiah has predicted, the Babylonian army invades and lays siege to Jerusalem (Jer. 38–39). The leaders in Jerusalem, rather than listening to Jeremiah, instead accuse him of treason, and lower him down into a muddy water cistern, ostensibly to let him die there. At this point in the story, no one in Jerusalem believes the word of God spoken by Jeremiah or stands up for him. His message is ignored and he is left to die in the cistern as the Babylonian siege rages.

An unlikely hero emerges at this point. A man named Ebed-Melech, identified repeatedly as a Cushite (i.e., a black African from the region along the Nile south of Egypt), confronts King Zedekiah and obtains permission to rescue Jeremiah from the cistern, probably saving the prophet's life. Soon Jerusalem falls to the Babylonians, who then execute most of the leaders who had opposed and persecuted Jeremiah. At this point God makes a clear statement about the fact that Ebed-Melech will live and be delivered because of his trust in God (Jer. 39:15–18).

In essence, God does for Ebed-Melech precisely what He would not do for King Zedekiah and the other leaders of Jerusalem—save him from the Babylonians. The contrast is stark, and in this context Ebed-Melech plays an important theological role in the story. At a time when all of Jerusalem has rejected the word of God—thus falling under His judgment—this Cushite foreigner trusts in God and finds deliverance. Ebed-Melech, a black African, stands as a representative for those Gentiles who will be incorporated into the people of God by faith.

There is a tendency among white Christians to view the biblical story as primarily a story about them (white people), with people of other ethnicities either absent from the story or added on peripherally later in the story. In reality, the story of Israel is a multiethnic story. The ancient Hebrews are a mix of ethnicities, with continual influxes of other nationalities. At the center of this trend is Moses' marriage to a Cushite woman. Likewise, at a very critical juncture in the story, it is the Cushite Ebed-Melech who emerges as the example and representative of the future inclusion of Gentiles who will be added to the people of God based on faith.

What Do the Gospels and Acts Say?

One of the central themes introduced in the Gospels and brought to the forefront of the story in Acts is that the gospel is for all peoples and ethnicities. There are numerous allusions in the Gospels to the Abrahamic promise in Genesis regarding the blessings that will come through Abraham and his descendants to peoples and nations (Gen. 12:3; 22:18). Likewise the Gospel of Matthew closes with the Lord's command to "go and make disciples of all nations" (Matt. 28:19 NIV). Also significant is the observation that Matthew 1 includes several interethnic marriages in the genealogy of Jesus. Tamar and Ruth were Canaanites, while Ruth was a Moabitess. The ethnicity of Bathsheba is not known, but she was married to a Hittite named Uriah, so possibly she was also a Hittite. The point of mentioning these foreign women in the genealogy of Jesus is to highlight the mixed nature of Jesus' lineage, suggesting and alluding to the upcoming Gentile mission and speaking to the readers of their responsibility to cross cultural and ethnic boundaries to spread the gospel.[4]

Luke and Acts in particular are especially concerned with developing this theme of Gentile inclusion and the crossing (or obliterating) of cultural or ethnic boundaries between peoples with the gospel. In the parable of the Good Samaritan (Luke 10:25–37), for example, Jesus teaches that loving your neighbor as yourself means loving those in particular who are different than you ethnically. That is His point in using the ethnically explosive Judean-Samaritan situation for the background of His parable. At this time the Judeans and Samaritans hate each other and ethnic tensions between them are high. Yet Jesus tells the story to a Judean audience with the Samaritan as the hero, clearly teaching His audience that "loving one's neighbor" meant crossing ethnic lines and caring for those who were ethnically different. Jesus also explicitly mentions crossing this same ethnic and cultural boundary in His marching orders to His disciples in Acts 1:8, "You will be My witnesses in Jerusalem, in all Judea *and Samaria*, and to the ends of the earth" (HCSB, italics added).

Continuing with this theme, as the Jewish leaders in Jerusalem reject the message of Christ and begin openly persecuting the apostles, Acts 8 presents the story of how an Ethiopian believes in the gospel and is saved. The term translated as "Ethiopia" in the New Testament refers to the exact same region that "Cush" refers to in the Old Testament. Similar to Ebed-Melech the Cushite in Jeremiah 38–39, this Ethiopian in Acts 8 believes the word of God proclaimed by the prophets and trusts in God, thus finding salvation, in contrast to the leaders back in Jerusalem. As the first Gentile believer in Acts, this Ethiopian serves as the forerunner or model representative of the coming Gentile inclusion, much like the role of Ebed-Melech in Jeremiah.

What Does Paul Say?

At the center of Paul's theology is the doctrine of justification by faith. That is, believers are forgiven their sins and are justified before God by the grace of God through faith in Christ. Yet Paul also develops the consequential and practical outworking of this doctrine. Since we all come before God based on what Christ has done for us rather than what we have done, then we are all equal before Him. Paul stresses this in passages such as Galatians 3:28, "There is no Jew or Greek, slave or free, male or female; for you are all one in Christ Jesus" (HCSB). The slightest notion of ethnic superiority is a denial of the theological reality of justification.

Furthermore, Paul's emphasis is not just on equality, but on unity. Thus in Colossians 3:11 he writes, "In Christ there is not Greek and Jew, circumcision and uncircumcision, barbarian, Scythian, slave and free; but Christ is all and in all" (HCSB). Likewise in Ephesians 2:14–16, Paul stresses that, in Christ, groups that were formerly hostile (like the Jews and Gentiles) are now brought together in unity in one body.

Paul is not just commending toleration of other ethnic groups in the church; he is teaching complete unity and common identity among the groups. He proclaims that we are all members of the same family, parts of the same body. Once we have been saved by faith and brought into Christ, then our perception of our self-identity must change, leading to a radical shift in thinking about other groups of people within the faith as well. Our primary identity now lies in the fact that we are Christians, part of Christ and His kingdom. This overshadows and overrides *all* other identities. Thus the primary identity for us, whether we are white Christians or black Christians (or Asian or Latin American, etc.) is that we are Christian ("in Christ"). This should dominate our thinking and our self-identity. We should now view ourselves as more closely related to Christians from other ethnicities than we are to non-Christians of our own ethnicity. We don't just tolerate each other or "accept" each other; we realize that we are connected together into one entity as kinfolk, brothers and sisters of the same family, united and on equal footing before God, and only because of what God has done for us. This does not obliterate the reality of skin color or cultural differences. What it changes is where we look for our primary self-identity. Our ethnic distinctions should shrink to insignificance in light of our new identity of being "in Christ" and part of His family.

How Does the Biblical Story End?

This unity is brought to a climax in the book of Revelation. Central to the climactic consummation presented in Revelation is the gathering of multiethnic groups around the throne of Christ. Revelation 5:9 introduces this theme by proclaiming that Christ has redeemed people "from every tribe and language and people and nation." This fourfold grouping (tribe, language, people, nation) occurs seven times in Revelation (5:9; 7:9; 10:11; 11:9; 13:7; 14:6; 17:15). In the symbolic world within the book of Revelation the number four represents the world while the number seven represents completion. Thus the seven-fold use of this four-element phrase is an emphatic indication that all peoples and ethnicities are included in the final gathering of God's redeemed people around His throne to sing His praises.[5]

Conclusion

The main points of this study can be synthesized into the following points:[6]

- The biblical world was multiethnic, and numerous different ethnic groups, including black Africans, were involved in God's unfolding plan of redemption.

- All people are created in the image of God and, therefore, all races and ethnic groups have the same equal status and equal unique value.

- Interethnic marriages are sanctioned by Scripture when they are within the faith.

- The gospel demands that we carry compassion and the message of Christ across ethnic lines.

- The NT teaches that as Christians we are all unified together "in Christ," regardless of our differing ethnicities. Furthermore, our primary concept of self-identity should not be our ethnicity, but our membership as part of the body and family of Christ.

- The picture of God's people at the climax of history depicts a multiethnic congregation from every tribe, language, people, and nation, all gathered together in worship around God's throne.

Discussion Questions

1. How does race and diversity relate to being created in the image of God?
2. Why does the Bible put such a value on diversity?
3. So much of the New Testament is written in the context of conflict about ethnicity. What mandate does the gospel put on us as Christians to pursue unity amongst diversity?

CHAPTER

2

What Does the Gospel Say?

Thabiti Anyabwile

IF WE ARE GOING TO DO THE WORK OF RACIAL RECONCILIATION, we need a robust doctrine of the image of God.

I want to offer a fuller understanding of this biblical idea and how that idea shapes the way we think about racial reconciliation. There are four phases of this.

First, we want to think about the original creation and what it means to be *made in God's image.* Second, we want to think about the distorted reflection and what it means for sin to have entered the world. How does this affect the way we bear God's image and likeness? How does this affect racial reconciliation? Third, we want to think about our re-creation in the image of God as Christians and how the redemption of Christ has a lot to say about how we pursue racial reconciliation. And fourth, we want to think about our final bearing of the image, glorification, and how we will reflect the likeness of God perfectly.

We Are Made in the Image of God

> Then God said, "Let us make man in our image, after our likeness. And let them have dominion over the fish of the sea and over the birds of the heavens and over the livestock and over all the earth and over every creeping thing that creeps on the earth." So God created man in his own image, in the image of God he created him; male and female he created them. (Gen. 1:26–27)

In a theological discussion there are many viewpoints regarding what it means to be made in God's image. Some say it is best defined by the reference to dominion in Genesis 1:26. Others point to the communicable attributes of God: characteristics of God that humanity shares. While others argue for a more specific idea like the capacity to love. Before turning to what I think it means specifically, let's consider a few basic things from Scripture.

Being made in the image of God sets us apart and distinguishes us from the rest of God's handiwork. We are the only image bearers of God in all of His creation. When you look at another person, whether male or female, you are beholding a creature that is a reflection of His image and likeness. Thus, gender is not merely a social construct, it is a divine construct connected with the image bearing of God.

C. S. Lewis wrote:

> There are no ordinary people; you have never talked to a mere mortal. Nations, cultures, arts, civilizations, these are moral and their life is to ours as the life of a gnat, but it is immortals with whom we joke, work, marry, snub, and exploit. Immortal horrors or everlasting splendors, this does not mean that we are to be perpetually solemn, we must play, but our merriment must be of that kind which exists between people who have from the outset taken each other seriously. No flippancy, no superiority, no presumption. We have never met mere mortals. Every person we have ever looked upon, smiled at, frowned at, greeted, encouraged, insulted, slandered, touched, is a person bearing the marks of divine likeness and the *Imago Dei*.[7]

Racial reconciliation must begin with the habit of seeing each other as made in the image of God; therefore, possessing inestimable, unfathomable dignity and worth. But how do we do that when seeing people is so commonplace? It requires skill and diligent practice. It requires renewing of our minds, especially with regard to racial identity.

Picture yourself walking into a cafeteria. You walk into the room and see two tables. One table is full of people from your ethnic background and another is full of people from a different ethnic background. You automatically think, *They don't look like me; therefore, we have nothing in common. It's not safe. I wouldn't have a good time with them.*

On the other side of the room, your mind does the opposite calculus. You see people who share your skin tone, and you think, *They're like me; therefore, we have a lot in common. It's safe. I should go over there and have a good time.*

The mind is a relentless stereotyper. In a fallen world it drives you away from the fundamental recognition that everybody you looked at in that room is like you, because everyone is created in the image of God. If we are going to rightly appreciate and practically embrace our common creation in the image of God, then we need a sure foundation: We need to break the habit of automatically stereotyping.

We Are Distorted by the Fall

We have to contend with the way the image of God has been distorted by the Fall. The world we now inhabit is not the world as God first made it. This world now suffers the corruption of sin. In Genesis 3, just two chapters after Creation, the Serpent tempts Adam and Eve and they sin against God; thus, subjecting all of creation to the effects of sin. In their disobedience to God, Adam and Eve plunged man into the knowledge of good and evil (Gen. 3:22)—a knowledge that was originally beyond the boundaries of proper human life. It's not good for us to know everything. We now know evil because they transgressed God's command and this knowledge sent the world spiraling into chaos.

In Genesis 4, Cain murdered his brother Abel. Fratricide is the result of the knowledge of good and evil. And in just a few generations, a man named Lamech (Gen. 4:19) participated in polygamy. In Genesis 4:24 he sought revenge and committed mass murder. Until we come to Genesis 6 when God looked down on humanity and the evil thoughts of their hearts. He sent the flood. He judged all of humanity and only saved eight souls. But even after the flood, we see chaos and sin. Natural questions arise: Is this the image of God? Is this the likeness of God? What happened to the image bearers?

In Genesis 9:6, God called on Noah and his sons to be fruit-ful and multiply. He follows that up with, "Whoever sheds the blood of man, by man shall his blood be shed" because "God made man in his own image." God gave a warrant for capital punishment, and the basis for that is the protection of the dignity and the reality that we are still image bearers of God. The image isn't completely lost, but it is distorted. The forces of sin in the world have been unleashed with a vehement desire to distort and extinguish that image. We live in a world bent on erasing the remembrance and the reflection of the Creator.

When it comes to racial reconciliation and the image of God, we have to be serious both about what it means to be made in the image of God as well as the seriousness of sin. Racial reconciliation cannot be achieved by people who deny original sin and the depth of human depravity. If we don't take sin seriously, we will be tempted to think that racism, racial animosity, prejudice, and bigotry are justifiable in some measure or eradicable by education alone. You cannot educate people out of racism, racial hatred, and animosity. This is why the practical Pelagian approach to racial reconciliation ends with so many people exhausted and frustrated. They misdiagnose how deep the problem is, so they use the wrong tools to address it. Mankind, though made in God's image, is corrupted at the root by sin.

We need a solution to racial strife that can reach the root of man's being. It is striking to me the number of Christians who, when talking about racial reconciliation, pull down the blinds and shutter up their souls. These Christians don't want to have a conversation about race for fear that they might expose themselves for having sinful racial thoughts or beliefs.

To be called "racist" is something people hate. In one sense, that's a sign of God's grace to us over the last fifty years. Decades ago being a racist was a respectable thing. But now it is a despised characteristic. Many Christians are so afraid of the label, the discussion, and the implications that they don't even want to have the conversation. The gospel frees us to joyfully admit our sins, face ugly things about ourselves, and to tell the truth about what's lurking in our hearts even when it's unpleasant. That's when we find hope.

King David wrote that when he refused to confess his sins, his bones groaned and he was in agony. But when he confessed his sins, he found freedom and relief. Confession can bring us freedom too. Confession would be a blessing in this fight for racial reconciliation.

What's the alternative? Pretend that these are not problems in our society? Pretend that we are not affected by racism or that it no longer exists? If racism does not exist, it will be the first sin produced by the Fall that was completely cured apart from the gospel. If racism does not exist, it will be the only form of alienation from the Fall to have vanished in the course of human history. We are only practicing self-deception if we think racism has vanished.

The potential for racism lurks in every heart, even if we have experienced a large measure of victory over it. We must be vigilant. We must set a guard over our hearts, minds, and mouths. If we don't, we are going to continue to be ill-equipped for this work of reconciliation. We are going to continue to find ourselves surprised and even upset and divided when racism raises its ugly head when we least expect. We must take seriously the reality and the deceitfulness of sin and protect God's image in one another if we want to see progress and racial reconciliation.

We Are Re-created in the Image of God

So what must we confess corporately and personally? We were created in the image of God, that image was distorted, but that's not the end of the story. We are told that we are re-created in His image if we are in Christ. Martin Luther wrote it this way in one of his hymns: "For still our ancient foe, doth seek to work us woe, his craft and power are great and armed with cruel hate on earth is not his equal." He went on to write: "The prince of darkness grim, we tremble not for him." Why do we not tremble in the face of satanic assault against the image of God and against the people of God? Luther explained it this way: "Did we in our own strength confide our striving would be losing. Were not the right man on our side, the man of God's own choosing, thus ask who that may be? Christ Jesus, it is He; Lord Saboath, His name, from age to age the same, and He must win the battle."

The battle Luther refers to is, of course, the work Christ completed on the cross. He Himself has become our peace.

He has reconciled us to God and to one another in his body on the tree. I love the words of Ephesians 2:16, "In one body through the cross, thereby killing the hostility." Christ has reconciled us to God through the cross. And in the process, he killed the hostility that once divided Jew and Gentile, and not only Jew and Gentile, but once divided Gentile and Gentile. He put it to death. The cross becomes a spear thrust through the heart of racial animosity and racial division.

How does the killing of hostility relate to the image of God, and how does it work out in our reconciliation? In Ephesians 4:17 Paul wrote: "Now this I say and testify in the Lord that you must no longer walk as Gentiles do, in the futility of their minds." In other words, we cannot live like unbelievers anymore. We must have our minds renewed to live differently. Verses 18–19 state: "[The Gentiles] are darkened in their understanding," and "alienated from the life of God because of the ignorance that is in them, due to their hardness of heart. They have become callous and have given themselves up to sensuality, greedy to practice every kind of impurity." But there is victory:

> But that is not the way you learned Christ!—assuming that you have heard about him and were taught in him, as the truth is in Jesus, to put off your old self, which belongs to your former manner of life and is corrupt through deceitful desires, and to be renewed in the spirit of your minds, and to put on the new self, created after the likeness of God in true righteousness and holiness. (Eph. 4:20–24)

We have been saved from the old way of life with its corruption and alienation. We must take off the old man and put on the new, which is *created after the likeness of God.*

This means that our reconciliation work is also sanctification work. We must pursue sanctification wherein Christ restores what sin distorted.

Christ has become our righteousness and our holiness. What was lost in the Fall is regained in Christ. There is a parallel passage in Colossians 3 that makes this connection even clearer and tells us more about what it means to embrace the likeness and image of God. Paul writes: "Put to death therefore what is earthly in you: sexual immorality, impurity, passion, evil desire, and covetousness, which is idolatry. On account of these the wrath of God is coming. In these you too once walked, when you were living in them" (Col. 3:5–7). Then in verse 8 Paul makes the contrast: "*But now* you must put them all away: anger, wrath, malice, slander, and obscene talk from your mouth" (italics added). All of these things can be expressed in our racial discord and prejudice. Paul continues in verses 9–10: "Do not lie to one another, seeing that you have put off the old self with these practices *and have put on the new self, which is being renewed in knowledge after the image of its creator*" (italics added).

Paul gives us the specific implication of this renewal in verse 11: "Here there is not Greek and Jew, circumcised and uncircumcised, barbarian, Scythian, slave, free; but Christ is all, and in all." Christ saved us from earthly unbelief. We are called to put away those old things that once divided us and put on a new self. The outworking of that new life, that renewal in knowledge, that regaining and restoring to the image of God, is this transethnic, transcultural, transreligious, and transeconomic unity we have in Christ. "In Christ there is not Greek and Jew." We are meant to live out these realities fully.

You cannot be a Christian renewed in the image of God and be indifferent or opposed to reconciliation in the body of Christ. Jarvis Williams put it this way, "Racial reconciliation is not an implication of the cross; it is the work of the cross."[8] This is not something that merely flows out of the cross as a secondary or tertiary application; this is what the cross produces. Christ has made, in Himself, one new man.

Do you have a place under the banner of Christian discipleship for renewing your mind on racial issues? Is that mind renewal central to what it means to be a Christian and a follower of Christ? If we don't, then we are liable to be opposing Christ and the unifying work of the Spirit. Sadly, it is possible to be born into a Christian family, converted at a very young age, live a long life, die and meet Christ, and in that entire span of our lives never have had someone sit down with us and systemically help us think about our new identity in Christ as it relates to racial issues and racial reconciliation. That's a problem. Particularly in a country and in a church whose greatest sin has been racism.

There is no Sunday school curriculum that teaches people how to rethink their identities in Christ. There are no popular Bible studies that address it. When we meet with our accountability partners, we don't usually hear questions such as, "Have you had any racist thoughts this week? Have you been thinking of your own identity in ways that look like the old man, rather than the new man that Christ has created?" It's not a part of our discourse. We are weak when the Fergusons erupt around us. We are weak when we watch Eric Garner choke to death on a city sidewalk. We don't know quite what to say or what to do when the U.S. Department of Justice reports tell us that an entire local police department and court system systematically mistreated and abused one ethnic group. We are immobilized because we are not discipled.

I want to encourage Christians to put the formation of new identities in Christ on our agenda because we are not doing the

Christian life well if we are not being sanctified in our thoughts about our identities and racial reconciliation.

Our Final Bearing of This Image

> See what kind of love the Father has given to us, that
> we should be called children of God; and so we are.
> The reason why the world does not know us is that
> it did not know him. Beloved, we are God's children
> now, and what we will be has not yet appeared; but
> we know that when he appears we shall be like him,
> because we shall see him as his is. And everyone
> who thus hopes in him purifies himself as he is pure.
> (1 John 3:1–3)

God tells us we are not just called the children of God, but that we *are* children of God. This is your divinely written biography. And it gets better. When we see Christ, we will be like him. That very act of seeing Christ glorified and coming for His bride completes the promise of Philippians 1:6: "He who began a good work in you will carry it on until completion, until the day of Christ Jesus." On the day of Christ Jesus, when we are made to see Christ with our very own eyes, the act of seeing Him will transform us into His likeness. The image we now bear in a clouded and shrouded way, we will bear perfectly when we are glorified together with Christ.

Conclusion

We have been made in God's image, and though we distorted that image with sin, we are redeemed by Christ. We are being conformed to His likeness and renewed in His image. And on the day He returns, the work of our glorification will be instantly completed as we behold him. If we take the doctrine of the image of God seriously, we will long for that likeness to be ours and shared with all other image bearers we see. Racial reconciliation rests upon this basis.

Discussion Questions

1. If the human mind is a "relentless stereotyper," how can an understanding of our common creation in the image of God correct the tendency to stereotype?
2. What role does sin play in our understanding of human identity?
3. How can the spiritual reconciliation achieved by Jesus on the cross affect efforts toward racial reconciliation?

CHAPTER

3

How Should the Christian Live?

Trillia Newbell

ANY ATTEMPT TO ENTER A CONVERSATION ON RACE AND ethnicity can leave even the bravest soul completely paralyzed. We tiptoe in fear wondering, *Can I say this? Should I say that? How will he respond if I ask about that?* What's the fear that reduces you to timidity and "safe" silence . . . being called insensitive, hurtful, or the worst: a racist? Conversations about race and ethnicity will not be going away any time soon. You and I have to engage it. And there are good reasons for why we should: the gospel reconciles us, we are the family of God, and it's truly a benefit to us, the church, and the world to display the race-transcending gospel.

As a child, I remember my parents telling me to obey them and when asked why, they simply answered, "Because I said so." They felt no need to inform me why I needed to obey them, they were the authority in my life and that was reason enough. Whether that tactic was the right one to take is neither here nor there, it worked for me. But I'm certain that if I took that approach to convince you that racial reconciliation should be pursued in your individual life, that wouldn't work so well. First, I have no authority in your life. Second, it's immensely important to know *why* it's an important pursuit for the Christian. It's God's Word that directs us, not me, and that makes all the difference. So, before I give you a list of practical steps that I think will assist you as we work toward reconciliation, let's first dive into understanding the why.

A Love for Neighbor

The increased use of social media has raised the visibility of the word *narcissism*. There isn't a day that goes by that I don't see narcissism referenced. Most people, quite honestly, seem to be throwing stones. You are a narcissist if you take a picture of yourself and post it onto social media. You are a narcissist if you post anything about yourself at all. Express your feelings: narcissist.

Picture with a friend: narcissist. Though I don't think it's good or right to constantly accuse others of narcissism, I do think there's some truth here. We are all narcissists. We can all just go ahead and say it, *I am a narcissist.*

Not the best admission, I know, but in order for us to truly love others, we've got to first be able to admit that we don't or, at the very least, it can be a struggle. Perhaps that's why Jesus said that we are to love our neighbor as ourselves (Mark 12:28–31). We see this again in Romans 13:8–10. Paul tells us that all commandments are summed up in this word, "'You shall love your neighbor as yourself.' Love does no wrong to a neighbor; therefore love is the fulfilling of the law.'" Of all of the commandments in Deuteronomy and Leviticus, the greatest is that we love our God with all our heart, soul, and mind, and love our neighbors as ourselves.

You might be thinking, *So what does this have to do with racial reconciliation?* Everything! While we know the commandment to love our neighbor, how often is it applied? And to be specific: How often is it applied to issues of race and ethnicity?

If God's greatest commandment for the Christian (after loving Him) is that we love one another, then we must begin there as we think through racial reconciliation. Love does no wrong to a neighbor, and most of the racial divides in our time are due to great wrongs. If we can gain an understanding of how to love our neighbors, then we can truly begin to pursue racial reconciliation. Even more fundamental than love, racial reconciliation begins with understanding our relationship between man and God and man to each other.

In the beginning God created *all* of mankind, male and female, in His image (Gen. 1:26). Before the foundation of the world, God, in His goodness and kindness, had His people in mind (Eph. 1:4). It was no surprise to our omniscient Father that Adam and Eve would fall and sin would enter the world. He knew people would not worship and delight in Him. And He didn't have to give us aspects of Himself, but He did. God—the holy one, pure and awesome—created us to reflect aspects of His beauty and character. We are not worthy of such a generous apportionment, but He gave regardless.

This alone should cause our hearts to leap for joy and pursue one another without hesitation. We are all created with the capacity to glorify God and know Him. We are all created equally. The Lord did not distinguish between the Christian and non-Christian in image bearers. And it is with that knowledge that the Christian delights to share the gospel.

Understanding our equality as image bearers changes everything we think about as it relates to our human relationships. As image bearers we should view others as God views us. One way the Lord identifies us—and I'd argue it's the most important—is whether we are in Christ or not.

This perspective should sharpen our focus to love, to reconcile, to pursue for the sake of the gospel. I've been the recipient of this kind of love; God sent a young girl aflame for Jesus and His gospel to share the Good News with me. I was not running after God, actually quite the opposite. My friend who shared the gospel with me was a young, wealthy white female and I was opposite in almost every way. What if she had allowed our differences in ethnicity to get in the way of the Great Commission to go and make disciples of all nations? Instead, out of her love for her neighbor, greater than her need for comfort, she pursued me and was able to share the gospel with me.

We love God because He first loved us and gave His Son to be a ransom for us (1 John 1:9). As you and I interact with others, we proclaim what we know about God through love for them and for God. Practically, in order to pursue racial reconciliation and ultimately the mission of God to make disciples of all nations, you must first ask God to give you a heart that loves others.

Get to Know the Family

Love is the answer for why to pursue racial reconciliation, but there's additional significance for the people sitting next to us in the pews. Racial reconciliation is a must because we are the family of God.

There is no denying the importance of family. My husband and children are my first priority and God's gift to me. When my husband is discouraged, it's a privilege to come alongside him and encourage him. When my kids are sick, my husband and I are there to nurse them back to health. Our relationships go much further than caring for one another, of course, but often these tangible expressions are the means of revealing the importance of the relationships. I imagine you would agree without hesitation that family is important. There's *another* family, often overlooked, that is of great value to the Lord—the family of God.

As Christians, you and I are adopted children of God. Paul tells us of our new bloodline when he writes: "The Spirit himself bears witness with our spirit that we are children of God, and if children, then heirs—heirs of God and fellow heirs with Christ, provided we suffer with him in order that we may also be glorified with him" (Rom. 8:16–17). We are children of God and a fellow heir with Christ. He created us and then He adopted us as His very own children. This includes everyone—every tribe and tongue and nation—who believes in the finished work of Jesus on the cross.

God doesn't discriminate based on ethnicity; He looks at the heart. *All* have sinned and fall short of the glory of God (Rom. 3:23). *All* are saved by faith alone through grace alone—left only to boast in Christ (Eph. 2:8–9). The gospel is for *all* nations.

We know this to be true, and yet so often we allow the differences in our skin color to dictate whether or not someone is accepted. God doesn't discriminate in His family. Racial reconciliation has been accomplished in Christ. There is no distinction. Those who trust in Christ for their salvation are adopted and, therefore, we are all brothers and sisters in Christ. We should be united in Christ. He's got a colorful family, and therefore so do we. Only in the family of God can people so distinctly different be the same (equal in creation and redemption) and counted as sisters and brothers in a new family. Knowledge and understanding of this new family and our adoption into it should be a wonderful motivator for pursuing one another in racial reconciliation and diverse friendships.

The Benefits of Relationship

I've covered some of the basic biblical principles for the pursuit of those not like us and the importance for racial reconciliation, so now let's think about the benefits. In his letter to the Corinthians, Paul recognized that there was great benefit in differences, namely (but not only) demonstrated through spiritual gifts. He shares in 1 Corinthians 12:12–26 about the benefit of each member of a church and their gifting by using the analogy of a body without hands or feet. The body functions fully and most effectively when each part is playing its essential role. Each member of the church is important and needed because God has generously given a variety of gifts.

The full context of the text in reference is about the function of the church, but the ideas can be applied to all of our lives. There is a benefit in knowing and interacting with others who are not just like you. And if you and I want to apply Paul's encouragement to the Corinthians, knowing others who are not like us allows for greater flourishing. We lose out when we stick with those just like us and—though this is *far* from exhaustive—I've been encouraged by the following six benefits to knowing someone different than you:

1. Serving

As already mentioned, one benefit of knowing those who are not just like you is that the family of God benefits from a variety of giftings. God intentionally did not make us all the same. God has given you and me spiritual gifts according to His great wisdom (Rom. 12:6). The purposes of these gifts aren't so that you can flaunt them or keep them for your own good—just the opposite (12:3). The purpose of your spiritual gifts is for the benefit of others. By knowing those who are not like us, we learn to serve others with the varied gifts God has given us for *their* benefit and *their* good.

2. A Taste of Heaven Now

Heaven will be filled with people from Indonesia, Dubai, Zambia, the Appalachian Mountains of East Tennessee, and the Grand Cayman Islands. Worshipping on the last day will include people speaking French, German, Spanish, English, Tagalog, and Arabic. And today we can get a foretaste of heaven when we step out of our comfort zones to get to know someone not like us.

3. Edification

Along with a variety of gifts, we all have different experiences. Life doesn't look the same for every person. Unless someone gets to know me, they'd never know that I traveled abroad, played the flute, or that I have had four miscarriages. God can use the unique experiences of others to encourage your faith, help you make decisions, or provide comfort. God's Word is filled with Scriptures encouraging us to build up one another. The Lord may just use that person who is not like you to bring the unique comfort you need from Him.

4. Racial Reconciliation

There's a rumor that, as a society, we are postracial, but the reality is not only are we not past racial divides, we continue to hear about division, racism, and tragic circumstances involving race throughout the country. Knowing others who are not like you is one way to display to the world that we are unified in

Christ through the gospel. It serves as a powerful picture of the transforming work of the gospel.

5. Gaining Understanding and Wisdom

Have you ever heard the term "ignorance is bliss"? It means that what you don't know won't hurt you. When relating to others, ignorance is not bliss; it's just plain old ignorance. Instead of remaining unknowing, you and I should instead strive to gain understanding through developing relationships with those not like us.

6. Seeing in Color

Imagine not being able to see color—it's a disorder that affects quite a number of people today. Unfortunately, it's a position regarding ethnicity that has been celebrated. Well-meaning and probably truly loving people use this phrase often, but I'd like to suggest that you are not color-blind, you don't need to be color-blind, and you should strive to not be color-blind. If you'd like to grasp the full beauty of God's creation, see color. Instead of pretending like we are color-blind, let's celebrate God's creation. Ethnic differences aren't the result of the Fall; celebrate the unique beauty of each and look forward to seeing heaven filled with the colors of all nations.

God intentionally created us unique. He could have made us all the exact same. He had the power to do that. Instead He chose to create you by name and with great thought (Ps. 139:13) and He delights over those He created (Zeph. 3:17). He has given each of us to one another to learn and grow from—this is His gift to us.

Faith in Action

So, by now, you're convinced. You realize that creation, redemption, adoption, and revelation prove that there is already a diverse kingdom. Throughout all of Scripture, from Genesis to Revelation, we see God working to redeem a people for Himself, a people from every tribe and tongue and nation—colorful and diverse. The pursuit of racial reconciliation and diversity reflects the Bible's description of the Kingdom. We pursue one another in love because the pages of Scripture are filled with it. And we pursue diversity because the gospel, the greatest news we will ever hear, embraces and advocates for a diversity of people to be born again into a new family for a holy and good God.

I've shared a few practical implications for our faith throughout the chapter already. As we understand the commandment to love our neighbors as ourselves, we understand that includes all ethnicities. We understand that the gospel is for all nations and, therefore, God's mission is also our mission so we strive to go and make disciples of all nations. We understand that God has a colorful, diverse family and, therefore, so do we as His adopted children. Getting to know Christians of other ethnicities is simply pursuing our family in love. And we realize that part of this means that we stop pretending to be color-blind, delight in God's creative design, and instead embrace our God-given differences.

Now What?

Perhaps you've been thinking about these topics for years, maybe even most of your life. Or maybe this is the first time you've considered how racial reconciliation affects you personally. It can seem daunting if your only reference or exposure to racial reconciliation is the Civil Rights Movement. Everyone isn't called in the same way. God doesn't call everyone to overseas mission and he didn't call everyone to march on the streets of Washington during the Civil Rights Movement. There were men and women who didn't leave their living rooms, who were never recorded in the history books, but who were still deeply engaged. You can do this right where you are. Isn't it good that God uses ordinary people to accomplish His mission?

Putting your faith in action with regards to racial reconciliation means you must be willing to: speak to your neighbor; gain knowledge; and see those around you. But you must also see that there's still a fight worth engaging. So often what hinders racial reconciliation is apathy to the topic of race. Apathy by definition is a lack of feeling, emotion, interest, and concern. It's a state of indifference, or even the suppression of emotions. We think that because the Jim Crow laws are now overturned, we have somehow magically become a society that is unified, equal, and desegregated. But just because we can now eat and drink and share pools by law doesn't mean that we are actually doing it or celebrating the image of God in each other. Because worship is available to us freely doesn't mean that we are choosing to join one another across racial lines. We are a society not willing to continue the fight because, from a legal standpoint, everything seems okay. So, we must take the action to speak to, know, and see our neighbor.

One of the problems from our apathy is that when people do rise up to discuss the continued racial struggles, concerns, and problems within our churches and society, many cry out that if we simply stop talking about race then all the struggles we see will disappear. I can understand why someone might think that bringing up the need for racial reconciliation can rebirth old wounds and, therefore, cripple the progress of racial reconciliation. The problem is, race continues to be talked about because there continue to be problems. And there continue to be problems because often conversations about race revolve around racism. And these conversations centered on racism happen because people are racist. So, until we see an end to racism, both personal and systemic, we will need to continue this conversation. And we can't brush off conversations about racial reconciliation because the gospel so clearly addresses it.

Because this conversation seems difficult, it is much easier to maintain the status quo rather than press into relationship and conversation with one another. But if we know that the gospel transcends race and we have the Spirit of God, we should be able and willing to take off the blinders that are hindering us from seeing the problem and the need for reconciliation. These conversations don't have to be difficult. We must take action to speak the truth in love and see our neighbors. This can be as simple as inviting someone to lunch.

A desire to suppress emotions can be at work here as well. We don't want to deal with the past, so instead of looking it straight in the face and standing arm-in-arm to deal with lingering hurt or learning from our past to continue a way forward, we want to forget about it. It's easier that way . . . the past is just too ugly. Slavery was an abomination and this country was built upon it. The unjust Jim Crow laws, separate but equal, were disgraceful, and our churches' history of using Scripture to justify sinful racism is grievous. But this is our history and regardless of the pain and emotion that might rise to the surface of your heart, it's worth engaging with our history for the purpose of unity and understanding.

We don't want to forget our shared history, we want to learn and grow from it. We want to understand how our past continues to affect communities today so that we can have informed conversations and equipped churches that are truly pursuing racial reconciliation. This isn't about guilt. No one should walk around feeling guilty for sin they did not directly commit. Rather it's about loving our neighbor as ourselves. Remembering the past will inform the future and will equip us for service to others. Remember, ignorance is not bliss; it's just ignorance. As you gain knowledge, you will feel less fearful of engaging in this conversation and, thus, racial reconciliation. So, you must take the action to gain knowledge so you can properly love your neighbor as yourself.

Conclusion

Gaining a biblical foundation is important as we pursue racial reconciliation. Understanding that it is a good thing in God's Word, rather than something trendy, helps us to be motivated to love and serve others not like us. We all need to reflect on our own apathy and ask the question: *Do I really care?* And then, we must die to ourselves, break free of our self-absorption, and learn about others. This will not only impact your own heart and soul but also the church. Be motivated out of a God-glorifying excitement for the diverse kingdom—that is already present in heaven and throughout the earth—to be displayed and enjoyed within your personal relationships.

My hope is that you can see that pursuing racial unity really isn't about diversity at all. It's about loving others. So as you step out in faith to get to know those who are not like you, it's not about quotas or because you *must*; rather be compelled by the love of Christ to love others as He has loved you. The power of the Spirit will enable you to pursue racial reconciliation. Pray that God would give you opportunities and that you will walk in boldness and surety in Christ as you seek to love your neighbor as yourself. Apart from Christ, you can do nothing. He provides the grace and the strength that you need.

Discussion Questions

1. Are you ever scared to ask questions about race and ethnicity?
2. How can "love for neighbor" motivate Christians to pursue racial reconciliation?
3. Why is "seeing in color" preferable to being "color-blind"?

CHAPTER

4

How Should the Church Engage?

Eric Mason

"Hip-Hop Has Done More for Racial Relations than Most Cultural Icons."

THIS STATEMENT WAS MADE BY JAY Z IN HIS LANDMARK interview with Oprah Winfrey on her OWN Network. Jay Z went on to say:

> "I think that hip-hop has done more for racial relations than most cultural icons. And I say, save Martin Luther King, because his dream speech we realized when President Obama got elected.

53

"This music didn't only influence kids from urban areas it influenced people all around the world," he says. "Racism is taught in the home. I truly believe that racism is taught when you're young, so it's very difficult to teach racism when your kid looks up to Snoop Doggy Dogg.". . .

"If you look at clubs and how integrated they have become—before people partied in separate clubs," Jay Z says. "There were hip-hop clubs and there were techno clubs. And now people party together and once you have people partying, dancing, and singing along to the same music, then conversations naturally happen after that. And within conversations, we all realize that we're more alike than we are separate."[9]

In many ways I agree with Jay Z. Hip-hop has broken amazing ground in creating a culture of institutions in which people of different ethnicities can join together and enjoy the artistic aspects of hip-hop culture. Inevitably, this cultural form has made its way into many spheres of the world. Several years ago, *National Geographic* did an article that highlighted the roots and global influence of hip-hop. There were people from the urban U.S. ghettos to Africa, Brazil, and Australia who all found themselves influenced in some way by the form. In it, people found belonging and community. With the influence of hip-hop have come expansive opportunities for people to develop natural self-improvement beyond the dreams of its founder Kool Herc and some of its noted architects.

When I look at this cultural genre and its impact, I can't help but find myself admiring and even being jealous in some ways. Yes, I have been deeply influenced by hip-hop culture, but I have been comprehensively transformed by the renewing power of the gospel. On November 15, 1992, I trusted Jesus Christ as my Savior and believed that His death on the cross was sufficient to transfer me from spiritual darkness to light (Col. 1:13–14). I truly believed that I was in a new family. However, the further I got in the church and was confronted with the gospel, I knew that there were many hills I had to climb as a believer. It wasn't until I moved out of a predominantly African American context in Washington, DC, and went to Dallas, Texas, and entered seminary that I learned I would have a new group of issues to face. Heading to seminary I had my mind blown in systematic theology classes, Hebrew, Greek, historical theology classes, Bible exposition, and other classes. I thought I had questions, but the classroom expanded the questions that I had. Furthermore, the new environment I was in totally awakened me to a new culture of Christianity. I had never seen churches the size of the ones I saw in Texas. If you had a thousand people at your church, that was considered minute. I saw churches with bowling alleys, movie theaters, roller-skating, video games, and large spaces for youth ministry that many churches would covet as space for their whole congregation.

As I began to look around, it was clear to me that with all of these resources, facilities, and people, there wasn't much cross-pollination or connectivity between the ethnicities. During this season I saw many great attempts by men and women to foster opportunities for racial reconciliation. Most began and ended with great hopes at fostering racial reconciliation, but to be honest, I don't think we knew or know today how and what reconciliation looks like.

These churches had resources that I hadn't dreamed a church would have. CEOs and millionaires from many sectors filled these ministries. The resources were so great that complacency could easily become a reality. In those types of settings, it takes great prophetic fervor to see a new movement started. The type of fervor and fearlessness found in Samuel, Elijah, Elisha, Daniel, Paul, John the Baptist, and even our Lord Jesus Christ. That was the midnineties and we still need it even more today.

In the wake of the many perceived justice issues between police and the African American community, it is clear to me that the responses of people across ethnic lines within the evangelical church signal a problem. The problem for me is that race relations are a major issue in the church. If we are going to honor the living God we have to, on some level, be of the same mind (Phil. 2). Our minds, across racial lines, are so splintered that there is a desperate need for the church to move toward a godly resolve on these matters.

The Biblical Mandate for Reconciliation

Paul makes it clear that we have been given the ministry of reconciliation (2 Cor. 5). What is reconciliation? One lexicon states, "reestablishment of an interrupted or broken *relationship*."[10] Without Jesus, we have a broken relationship with God and one another. However, the gospel restores our relationship with God and one another. Positionally, we are restored with one another, but practically we have to deal with the breakdowns that impede our attempts at reconciliation. Therefore, unity takes commitment on all fronts. At the core of reconciliation is the fact that Jesus dealt with our offense holistically before the living God. What aliened us from God and what alienated us from one another, and that which has caused hostility, has been crushed through Jesus.

Reconciliation requires the restoration of friendly relationships and of peace where before there had been hostility and alienation. Ordinarily, it also includes the removal of the offense which caused the disruption of peace and harmony to begin with. This was especially so in the relation of God with humanity, when Christ removed the enmity existing between God and mankind by acting as a sacrifice on our behalf. The Scripture speaks first of Christ's meritorious, substitutionary death in achieving the reconciliation of God with sinners; of sinners appropriating this free gift by faith; the promised forgiveness and salvation that become the sinners' possession by grace; and, finally, reconciliation to God (Rom. 5:10; 2 Cor. 5:19; Eph. 2:16).[11]

Moreover, as a church, Jesus motivates us to engage in reconciliation as a part of our identity as ambassadors. As a church, we must face what has brought and continues to nurture hostility between the ethnicities. Saying, "Get over it!" is an affront to the spirit and heart of reconciliation. Reconciliation means we face our issues with one another knowing that God offers grace to deal with our racial division through the power of Christ.

Blacks must not be apathetic, and whites must not be dismissive. These two issues in the fight for reconciliation have equally been hurtful in dealing with God's desired ends for using Jesus Christ. In the recent days, issues in our country—from the Travon Martin case to Eric Garner's—many (not all) whites have shown an unparalleled amount of insensitivity that has created deeper breaches in the church and deepened the apathy of African Americans toward racial reconciliation.

The apathy that I have seen has been in the ratio of black persons at gatherings organized around racial reconciliation over the years. Most events have had a minimum of 85 percent white attendance and others are just about entirely white. As I have surveyed pastors, however, they feel as though there is no desire on the part of our white brothers and sisters for a deeper understanding and commitment to reconciliation, despite high attendance at such events. As justified as African Americans may feel to walk in apathy, we can't if there is an authentic commitment by our white brothers and sisters to seek clarity to know what to own, and repent in order that repentance may take place. Even if we feel like we've done all that we could to be at peace as Romans 12 communicates, we must leave the door open for the Spirit of God to work. In addition, whites must see engaging the blind spots that exist in their sphere pertaining to race as a systemic application of the gospel in our contemporary society today.

Treating Race as a Sanctification Issue

At the end of the day, this issue is a spiritual growth issue. Ephesians 4 speaks of unity that helps the church as a whole to become one new man in Jesus as a fully grown community to represent His Excellency to the world. Refusing to reconcile when there is an issue brought forth or if the willingness to repent is present, we sin by rejecting the opportunity to bridge that gap. We had an event at our church that we opened up to the nation called "Nationwide Solemn Assembly," where we called the church to engage in a time of fasting and praying through this issue. Our church facility had standing room only where we saw Latinos, Asians, African Americans, Africans, whites, and people from the Caribbean come together to seek the face of God through fasting and praying. A white man came to the microphone to talk and confessed that his wife made him come. He stated that he was a staunch racist and needs to work through what he should do now as a Christian. The impact of his confession was haunting and refreshing. You could feel that he is still deeply racist against the black community, but he admitted that hearing the heart of African Americans that night and the legacy of systemic racism was causing him to repent of the biases he learned when he was a young child and young man.

Treating Race as an Issue of Spiritual Warfare

The first full week of every year we call a "Solemn Assembly" and declare a time of fasting and seeking the living God on different areas in our lives where we need breakthroughs—for ourselves and over issues in the world. As the matters on race came up, we decided that it was paramount to fast and pray. As we began to get ready for it, we found people around the country wanting to join us in this effort to do the same. In assessing this, we found that we hadn't been treating racial reconciliation as a spiritual warfare issue. We understood as believers based on Ephesians 6 that we don't wrestle against flesh and blood, but many times, on the issue of race, we have thrown solutions at this complex issue that are good, but we've not gotten to the root of the problem—which is a heart beset by sin. In short, we have underestimated the role of spiritual warfare when it comes to racial reconciliation. We can't simply work to "overcome" this issue; we must view racial reconciliation as an act of warfare against powers and principalities that seek to keep Christ's church in a state of disarray. The Devil would love for us to continue to treat this matter on a natural plain because that is where he fights the best against us.

Churches need to recognize that one of the Enemy's devices is to fight against reconciliation between God's people (2 Cor. 2:11). Paul commands us not to be ignorant of Satan's devices. We might think of one of Satan's schemes as a stronghold that keeps us from achieving unity. In 2 Corinthians 10:4, "stronghold" is used. It is one of the things that Satan uses to exalt something else in the mind of the believer above that of the Lord Jesus Christ. A stronghold is a mind-set, value system, or thought process that hinders your growth, the growth of others, and prevents you from exalting Jesus above everything in your life and maximizing the fruitfulness that best aids in God's people bringing glory to the living God. Racism and hatred toward reconciliation are both strongholds. They are mind-sets that are beset in the life of the churches in our country and world that need to be pulled down.

However, Paul says, "For the weapons of our warfare are not of the flesh but have divine power to destroy strongholds" (2 Cor. 10:4). Divine power verses fleshly power. Even Paul is letting us know that any stronghold that we face must be done so with divine power. The gospel is the power of God and we draw strength from that gospel through seeking the face of the Lord to reveal and remove the demonic forces that war against the unifying identity of the people of God. We must not accept less than what the Lord wants.

What Racial Reconciliation Does Not Look Like

Diversity without Honesty

I happen to pastor a diverse church. Epiphany Fellowship has people from all over the map. The issue, however, is that there isn't yet a breakthrough of diversity in anything else but Sunday morning, staffing, and college ministry. We are growing in this, but our diversity must be stronger in our small groups. Whenever I challenge this, people are very apathetic. When we, as a church, had to challenge the race issues that the world was facing, only the minorities came out in strong numbers, but our other brothers and sisters of the majority culture didn't show a strong interest. Only a few faithful did so. And the people that came struggled with the honesty that particularly African Americans wanted to voice. Several of the people in our church that were age fifty and older shared their stories of brutality and it was clear that they suffered from sort of a post-traumatic stress disorder from the history of racism in America. So the events that were coming up only surfaced the lack of healing that they felt hadn't happened. Their desire is that a multiethnic church would be the environment by which they could see this longing fulfilled.

Trying to Hire Reconciliation

I can't tell you how many brothers in Jesus that I receive calls and e-mails from who want me to point them toward solid African American guys that they can hire. Most of them, but not all of them, want to hire a guy who would be the mascot of diversifying the church they pastor. There's good motive behind this, but it's a bad approach, because it fails to consider what real diversity entails. Diversity has to be geographically available to you and it has to be a part of our lives on a regular day-to-day level. Nothing is wrong with hiring a diverse staff, but that won't deal with the systemic brokenness in race relations through the church. To be honest, it can make it worse. Many ethnic minorities that I know of in this scenario are frustrated on several levels, and the church that hired them as support staff realizes that they hired based on color, not the most qualified. Then they are in a bind because they are fearful of firing the guy or gal they expected to move the church forward in diversity. It's a mess!

Forcing a Church into Multiethnicity

Church planting was the sexy thing that everyone had been running toward, but now it is multiethnic churches. I highly applaud my brothers and sisters in Christ who want diversity. I want diversity and seek it in the church. However, when people read in Revelation of how the future age includes people ransomed from "every tribe and language and people and nation," and we think we can perfectly achieve that now, we can do great damage.

What do I mean?

Many who go here say the church must look like heaven; therefore, all churches must be multiethnic. It is a nontransferable dangerous expectation contextually. Making this a universal reality for every local church isn't only unbiblical, but also impossible. Many brothers longing for diversity push their congregations toward this while being in a state, county, town, city, or neighborhood that is homogeneous. Because of this, diversity isn't going to be a practical reality for that local church. Multiethnicity is a good thing but it isn't a demand or reality for every church. What matters is that every church remains open and embracing of all persons who are their brothers and sisters in Christ, regardless of skin color.

Even in cities where there are multiple people groups, multiethnic ministry may not take root. In complex urban realities like Boston, New York, and Philadelphia, multiethnic churches could pose a larger obstacle missiologically because of the neighborhood's composition. Neighborhood cities sometimes need homogenous churches because of how complex people groups are to reach. In Boston, there are Cambodian, Ethiopian, and Portuguese churches. When there are first-generation realities that are being faced, just to learn how to incarnate the gospel among that one group is hard enough; it would be a challenge to forcefully engage in multiethnic ministry because such engagement might be presumptuous and overlook the sensitivity that each ministry context demands.

Engaging the church in a multiethnic way should be encouraged in contexts where there is a homogenous crossroad. Even when you look in Scripture, Hellenistic culture spread throughout the Middle East, allowing for people of different cultural backgrounds to have common ground to understand and share cross-culturally. When I look at the Bible, particularly the New Testament, I am encouraged that the church was the innovator of diversity. The gospel, churches, and missionaries were adept to cross-cultural ministry that understood navigating the challenges of the complex milieu.

Apparently, the pervading presence of Hellenism after the conquest of Palestine by Alexander the Great in 332 BC posed a more serious challenge. Hellenism presented itself as a higher culture, with great richness and strong allure. Greek culture was not wholly bound up with traditional Greek religious thought. It was also a literature, a philosophy, and ethics. Over the course of time a form of Judaism even developed that included Hellenistic values, showing that many Jews considered Hellenism to be reconcilable with their religious beliefs.[12]

Ministering in this way means that to do ministry cross-culturally, we can connect to the redeemable components within our multifaceted subcultures. That is why Jesus gives Matthew 28:18–20 and Acts 1:8, because He expects His gospel to penetrate every culture and people, and it could include bringing some of those individual cultures into the same local community for worship and mission. The goal is making disciples, not our personal dreams that may work against disciple making.

Some Places to Start

Church Leadership

Church leadership must own reconciliation. If the leadership doesn't, the church will not either. In Acts 15, the mother church of Jerusalem had to wrestle with race issues. They had to wrestle through whether Gentiles could be saved and, if so, how should they be discipled. Led by the apostles and the elders, there was a plan of action to intentionally inform them of cultural and theological distinctives which would help aid in the gospel potently moving along in multiethnic territories. This would keep the door open for racial reconciliation between the Jews in the regions where the Gentiles were coming to faith. If Jews were to be engaged, there had to be racial sensitivity to their experience among the Gentiles in their history. In essence, that is why the letter was sent for circulation in Gentile territory.

Pastors must challenge the church beyond its comfort zone to face its substandard views of the *Imago Dei* and God's Word. One of the ways we have accomplished this is to bring together pastors from ethnic lines to take the initiative into our churches and to fight for the unity of faith (Eph. 4). Over sixty pastors across ethnic and denominational lines have responded. More pastors are getting connected to pray and work hard to bridge the obvious gaps we have between one another. Our meeting was simple: it consisted of prayer and honest dialogue on race. We are hoping to be more honest with one another as time persists.

Grow the Racial I.Q. in the Church

One of the things I am working with the pastors in our area to do is help strengthen our understanding of one another ethnically and socially. Therefore, we are doing a summit with all of our local churches coming together to consistently enter into dialogue. Professors in sociology and history from our churches will help us navigate the difficult sociological terrain. In addition, the people within our churches will enter relational dialogue to work through the challenges we feel. It's going to be tough, but the work is needed.

Engaging the City

Also, I have tasked several of our brothers with developing a larger summit in the city. We will call on the police leadership, city government, and people in our neighborhoods from different backgrounds to come together and talk as well as look for solutions. These solutions would involve how we can work to rebuild trust between law enforcement and minority communities. Our desire is to see the church live out Ephesians 3 and Jeremiah 29:3–9 in our cities.

Unity Worship Gathering

Finally, we want to do a unity Sunday morning gathering. This would involve all of the churches meeting one Sunday morning together at one of the large arenas in the city. We would have multiethnic service, worship, and preaching together. We can't wait for this opportunity.

All of the above is just the beginning of helping us all to think through what it would mean to intentionally pursue reconciliation through the church where we live and dwell within the life of the local church. It doesn't promise to be easy. Likely, there will be pain, difficulty, and some awkwardness as we pursue an objective that is strained in the society we live in. Our hope is to see there be systemic gospel change through the church of Jesus Christ. Instead of us arguing about race issues, we become agents of reconciliation to the glory of God through Jesus Christ.

Discussion Questions

1. What are some of the common mistakes made by churches pursuing racial reconciliation?
2. What can the early church teach us about being intentional in the areas of race and reconciliation?
3. What are some practical steps churches can take to facilitate reconciliation within their congregation and community?

CHAPTER

5

What Does the Culture Say?

Matthew J. Hall and D. A. Horton

Ben Affleck made headlines in the spring of 2015 when news broke that he had requested producers of PBS's *Finding Your Roots* program omit the discovery of slave-holding ancestors in his family.[13] The sense of shame the actor, director, and activist felt was understandable. And the outrage that he would seem to attempt to hide the truth of his own family's history was equally understandable. In some small way, the whole controversy reminded us that we still have a hard time speaking truthfully about the past in a manner that will foster true reconciliation.

American evangelicals have a lot of raw nerve endings exposed when it comes to talking about race. The slightest provocation inflames our passions and we are quick to delegitimize any perspective different from our own. We do this, in part, by refusing to speak honestly about the past and to learn from it. And if we are unwilling to look at the past with honesty, it is virtually impossible that we are prepared to speak truthfully and empathetically about the present.

Why Racism Is Ancient *and* Modern

In one sense, the roots of racial hierarchy are as old as the book of Genesis. Human civilizations have always, because of the very nature of sin, been prone to the temptation to elevate the identity of their community and culture over that of outsiders. However, our understanding of race is also historically tied to the modern age, forged in the fires of the scientific revolution and the transatlantic slave trade. And, at its core, it has been theological since, quite often, modern arguments defending slavery and racial hierarchy were framed in theological terms.

And, of course, our contemporary American problems of racism, inequality, and injustice extend far beyond binary categories of black and white. This is, in part, due to the realities of a wide range of historical developments and ideologies that resulted in everything from Indian removal and Asian exclusion to flagrant xenophobia and nativism.

But there is a reason that our conversations surrounding race, reconciliation, and justice often seem to hinge on categories of blackness and whiteness. While we should not exclude or minimize the necessity of reconciliation among all of God's people, American evangelicals continue to wrestle with the long and horrific legacy of slavery and a society that identified blackness with inferior status, limited opportunity, and minimal legal protection.

The call to be reconciled to one another in Christ makes specific and contextualized demands upon Christians in various places and at various times. That is because human beings have a remarkable and sinful propensity to build all sorts of "dividing walls of hostility." In one corner of the planet it might mean that Christians are called to love their redeemed brothers and sisters from another ethnic or socioeconomic group that they would naturally be directed to hate, oppress, or even kill. For example, the gospel will demand that redeemed Tutsi and Hutu be reconciled to one another, even when the world says they should slaughter one another. The same gospel would call converted Jews and Palestinians to understand their kinship in Christ by faith and to be reconciled. In our contemporary American context, white and black evangelicals continue to wrestle with the trauma of centuries of racialized violence, injustice, and evil.

So while racial reconciliation involves far more than black and white conflict in the United States, it continues to pose a prime and urgent demand for gospel witness within the context of American evangelicalism.

We should also plainly note that the way we often think about race itself is largely a modern and fallacious one. Whereas a variety of historical forces redefined race into a biological category in the early modern period, we must affirm that race is an idea, a public myth, and a social currency. What makes someone "white"? Think about it. And what criteria make someone "black"? Race is not about biology, but ideology. Thus, categories of blackness and whiteness have always been negotiable and fluid, able to be leveraged in different ways at different times to wield power and to construct hierarchical systems. The categories of blackness and whiteness thus have a long and complex history, one tied to questions of power and justice. As sociologist Michael Emerson has pointed out, American evangelicals continue to live in a "racialized society," one in which "race matters profoundly for differences in life experiences, life opportunities, and social relationships."[14] So how did we get here?

Racism Made in America

While race is both ancient and modern, our contemporary experience in the United States has been shaped by the unique story of slavery and racial hierarchy. Quite simply, if you live in the United States you cannot escape the reality of our very American version of race and racism. Contested theological visions have also complicated the story. For our own denomination, the Southern Baptist Convention, this story is particularly painful. Like many white Protestants, our history is one that is inextricable from the legacy of racial hierarchy, slavery, and Jim Crow.[15]

The way in which Americans experience race is historically informed, rooted in the realities of colonization, labor, geography, and theology. While the transatlantic slave trade implicated virtually every European colonial power—including the Portuguese, Dutch, French, English, and Spanish—the circumstances were especially opportune in the British colonies for an entire racialized worldview to take hold, one legitimizing the involuntary trafficking of black African bodies.[16]

Of course, in time, the theological worldview that legitimized racialization and enslavement was contested. Ministers and theologians, both black and white, increasingly called into question the assumptions and exegetical arguments proposed by defenders of racial hierarchy and slavery.[17] Even after a bloody Civil War and emancipation, American culture—including evangelicalism—struggled to come to terms with the horrors of racial violence, injustice, and wickedness not only in the Jim Crow South, but throughout the nation.

So it is no small providence that it was also theology that animated the Civil Rights Movement. If theology served to prop up and perpetuate racial injustice, it was also a profoundly theological vision that drove the courageous efforts of those calling for freedom and justice. While some appealed to poorly constructed exegetical arguments from the Bible to defend segregation and the racial status quo of Jim Crow, the Civil Rights Movement articulated a vision for "beloved community," one where the Old Testament vision of justice, righteousness, and love were prioritized.[18]

Explicitly theological arguments for racial segregation were not uncommon, even well into the 1950s. For example, significant numbers of evangelicals appealed to a smattering of passages to denounce interracial marriage. Arguing that God had deliberately created separate races out of humanity and had intended them to be separate (even going as far as placing them on separate continents), they concluded that it would be against God's divine will to allow "racial amalgamation."

One of the most common arguments to defend the enslavement of black persons was an embarrassingly poor interpretation of Genesis 4. Concluding that the "mark" God placed upon Cain in judgment for the murder of his brother, Abel, denoted some kind of racial identity or skin color, some used this to conclude that black skin represented the mark of Cain. More commonly, some appealed to the Tower of Babel account in Genesis 11,

arguing that the story implied the necessity of racial differentia-
tion—and segregation. Perhaps the most common was from the
story of Noah's sons in Genesis chapters 9 and 10. After one of
his sons, Ham, observes Noah drunk and naked, then mock-
ingly reports the episode to his brothers, the patriarch calls forth
a curse upon his grandson, Canaan: "Blessèd be the LORD God
of Shem; and Canaan shall be his servant. God shall enlarge
Japheth, and he shall dwell in the tents of Shem; and Canaan
shall be his servant" (Gen. 9:26–27 KJV).

By the 1830s, this passage had been appropriated wholesale
by proslavery apologists, tying the curse to blackness. Even after
emancipation, these stories continued to be employed to justify
racial hierarchy. While slavery had been legally dismantled, the
story of the dispersion of Noah's sons in Genesis 10–11 now
shifted to be employed as an argument for racial segregation.[19]

If Southern Baptists—and evangelicals in general—are
going to get this right, we need to also be honest about where
we have gotten it wrong. Whitewashing our own history helps
nothing and no one; in fact, it only compounds evil. The truth
is some of our most eminent Baptist theologians appropriated
horrendous exegetical arguments to justify white supremacy. For
example, John Leadley Dagg, president of Mercer University,
claimed that "as the sons of Adam are bound to submit patiently
to the curse which requires them to earn their bread in the sweat
of their face, so the sons of Ham are bound to submit patiently

to the curse which has doomed them to bondage."[20] This history should chasten us. We hold fast to an inspired, inerrant, and infallible Bible that speaks authoritatively. But if our own ancestors in the faith could so grossly misapply portions of the Holy Scriptures, we should be mindful of our need for humility before the text and our constant need for illumination from the Holy Spirit.

Historical Truth Telling Matters More Than We Think

All of this would be nothing more than an interesting historical or sociological account if we did not go further. But the point of this for Christians—those reconciled to God through the atoning death of Jesus Christ—is that we are called to be reconciled to one another. And reconciliation requires truth telling, especially about the past.

But there is a problem. The more we talk to pastors and Christian laypeople, the more we hear of those who desire to be in churches, institutions, and communities that are diverse. We believe this is a sincere aspiration and it is one for which we should be deeply thankful to God. However, we fear that many white evangelicals want to arrive at the destination of diversity without walking the necessary path of reconciliation. And that path—one laid out for us in the message of the gospel—is one that requires telling the truth about sin. It requires intentionality, since true reconciliation never happens by accident.

Americans are especially susceptible to the naïve and damaging assumption that we can remove ourselves from our own history. When we talk about racial reconciliation, it is not uncommon to hear someone reply, "What in the world do I have to apologize for? I never owned slaves, never operated a segregationist lunch counter, never protested against desegregation . . . If I haven't done anything wrong, how can you say I need to be *reconciled*?"

It is not an entirely stupid question. But it betrays just how significant our challenge is. Embedded within a hyper-individualistic culture, we often lose sight of the ancient—and biblical—truth that we inhabit space *and* time and are deeply connected to one another, connected to history, and tied to all kinds of virtues and evils. We thus fail to account for the fact that sin has toxic implications not only for individuals, but for cultures, societal structures, and worldviews. Our own way of thinking, loving, hating, and feeling are shaped—often in ways of which we are even unaware—by this reality.

And if our churches have been complicit in the evils of racial injustice and hatred, there is also hope. The message of reconciliation has been deposited in the gospel of Christ, entrusted to the church, and proclaimed since the apostles. We are an imperfect bunch, to be sure, and we often have contradicted this gospel in our own imperfect, sinful, and broken ways. But the gospel is unchanged. It is "the power of God for salvation to everyone who believes" (Rom. 1:16), the message that tells of a God who reconciles sinners to Himself *and to one another*, tearing down the dividing walls of hostility. It is the same gospel that declares that Christ *Himself* is our peace (Eph. 2). And if that is the case, then the church is called to live out the reality of this settled peace, achieved through Christ's perfect life and atoning death and resurrection. As civil rights hero and Christian statesman John Perkins has put it, this is "a gospel that burns through racial and cultural barriers and reconciles people to God and one another."[21] The issue of racial reconciliation then becomes a matter of Christian discipleship, a vital part of what it means to follow and obey our Master. So how do we, as Christians, walk this path as those who have already been reconciled and are called to be reconcilers?

The church in America has a glaring past of poor stewardship of how the gospel relates to racism. Presently the body of Christ finds our work of racial reconciliation cut out for us. The culture of our day leverages the church's racial history as something it either *ignores* or *idolizes*. Yet, for believers, by being truthful about our past we can leverage it as a launching pad to move us forward toward biblical reconciliation. As God's chosen people, our life's mission is at the intersection of two passages: Matthew 28:19–20 and 2 Corinthians 5:17–21. We've been commissioned to make disciples of all ethnicities while living as new creations in Christ serving as God's ambassadors of reconciliation. Reconciliation between sinners and a Holy God evidenced through interpersonal harmony is our life's clarion call.

As is His track record, the Lord couldn't have called us at a better time. The United States is growing more ethnically diverse daily and God is allowing His bride to have another opportunity to represent Him well. Arguably, the church in America today, more so than any other generation in our nation's history, has been given a timely opportunity to lead the cultural conversation on racial reconciliation by personifying the answer. However, before we can lead, we first need to sweep around our own front door and follow it up by a thorough cleaning of our own house.

In order to change the cultural conversation on race, the church must gain credibility by having our lifestyle match the message of the gospel we proclaim. This can be achieved when we first take a *look* at our own individual sinfulness hiding in our hearts. Next, make intentional efforts to have ongoing honest interpersonal communication with local believers from different cultures, ethnicities, generations, and socioeconomic backgrounds. While we're engaged in sincere dialogue, we must *listen* to the hearts of those to whom we're speaking and posture ourselves to *learn* from them. These conversations are not to be on occasion; rather, ongoing so the body of Christ can *live* in unity. Finally, as we're witnessing Christ growing His body into maturity, the world will take notice and we'll be able to *lead* the national conversation on racial reconciliation.

Look

Our first step in this process is a truthful assessment of our own heart. Since we were all conceived in sin (Ps. 51:5) and from birth were natural liars (Ps. 58:3), we're prone to smoke screen our sinful racial prejudices. Humor is often the mask of choice for racist jargon because we use it as our attempt to wade in the water of race-centered conversations. The result of such a practice leads to the building of superficial relationships. The work put forth into sustaining superficial relationships quickly unravels in moments of conflict, the litmus test for every relationship.

In the midst of conflict our filters are removed, allowing the content of our heart to become known through what we communicate and our once light-truthful humor has mutated into hateful cynicism. Jesus was on to something when He said, "For the mouth speaks from the overflow of the heart" (Matt. 12:34 HCSB). Living in a fallen world guarantees continual moments of racial conflict until Christ's return. Sadly, what's been grievous to witness is the ungodly speech spewed between believers during moments of racial conflict. At times it's been hard to determine distinction between the culture's voice on race and the church.

In Psalm 139:23–24 David cried out for God to search him and know his heart in order to find the offenses there that served as hindrances of him walking upright. Far too often we react to conflict in similar fashion as the world because we're not modeling David by being proactive in asking God to surface the issues of heart in private before they spill out in public or through an inappropriate joke.

When God reveals our sin, we must confess them to Him so we can be forgiven (1 John 1:8–10). If God surfaces issues with race and prejudices toward others, we should go to those we have issues with, confess to them our sinfulness, and seek their forgiveness and reconciliation. At the same time, when we approach them, we must posture our hearts to hear the depth of their hurt and work to stay engaged with them for the long haul. The key to seeing this become reality is regular interpersonal communication.

Listen

Next we must honestly ask ourselves: What level of change will result from talks about race and the gospel with those who share our same ethnic background? How can we begin showing empathy and sympathy toward those in the body whose personal narratives include experiences far different from our own if we lack ongoing interpersonal communication with them? Although we're not people "of" the world, we shouldn't be so naïve to deny we still live "in" the world. The world we live in wants us to create enclaves of homogenous communities in order to maintain our preferred comfortable status quo.

The culture around us sets a rhythm of life conducive for homogony to be preferred when we talk about race.[22] Naturally, the human tendency is to gather with those who are like us, yet, for the body of Christ, we see God saves people from every nation, tribe, and tongue (Rev. 7:9), so diversity is in our DNA. The tension believers face is living as agents of both spiritual and racial reconciliation amidst a culture preferring segregation when dealing with race. It would do us well to assess our own personal network of interpersonal relationships to see how much diversity is present.

The reason being, when we are not in dialogue with people, we easily disconnect from their lives; and when one of their life decisions is made known to us, it's easy to make a judgment call on their decision by using our assumptions as evidence. Assumption reigns sovereignly where honest communication is absent. Without honest interpersonal communication between members of the body of Christ, we'll continue to sit in contentment with racial prejudice nestled in our heart. We must counteract this by being proactive in asking God to surface the issues of our hearts and then intentionally seek out interpersonal communication with those in the body of Christ who are different from us.

In his book *The Nature of Prejudice*, Gordon W. Allport advocates a position known as the Intergroup Contact Theory. In short, he believed through interpersonal contact, members of minority and majority groups could reach a common goal.[23] Through a series of testings, Thomas Pettigrew and Linda Tropp report 94 percent of their studies support Allport's theory.[24]

Allport's theory isn't groundbreaking for Christians since Christ Himself advocated interpersonal communication as it relates to personal faults, offenses, and the extension of forgiveness a couple millennia before Allport's work was published (cf. Matt. 5:21–24; 6:14–15; 18:15–17). Since the common goal for the body of Christ is reconciliation, we're at fault for not living this out if we're avoiding interpersonal contact with believers who are different from us. In our day, the culture around us wants us to substitute interpersonal communication with surface-level online engagement.

In large, we cannot control the diversity of the community we inhabit; however, the online communities we create are the perfect place to begin assessing our dedication to diversity as it relates to our interpersonal relationships. Studies have shown segregation exists inside the online communities we create.[25] Social media has created the potential for everyone's wobbly soapbox to expand into a worldwide platform. The world watches as believers spew venom at each other during national moments of racial conflict. These responses can be avoided if we have ongoing face-to-face dialogues and listen to the hearts of those we're in relationship with. In the body of Christ, we must work with diligence to hear our brothers' and sisters' hearts so we can learn their life narratives.

Learn

To have a heart that desires dialogue, it requires humility. Our goal is to enter the conversation with a heart of humility. This is a practice we suggest the body of Christ begins to employ before we engage interpersonally about race with other believers.

It takes great humility to create space that allows a person to unpack their personal life experiences we cannot sympathize with, while refraining from cutting them off, fact-checking them, accusing them of exaggerating details, or dump-trucking our personal takes from national moments of racial conflicts on their life experience. In the culture today, in public both on television and the Internet, there is great lack in the distribution of both empathy and sympathy. These are two blind spots Christians must intentionally focus on in order to show a countercultural response to race relations. For those who were not raised in an impoverished community, who have never been racially profiled, ridiculed because of their skin color, or felt the daily pressures of systemic oppression, they would do well to hear the hearts of the believers who express their painful experiences that include such details. Empathy is not allowing ourselves to travel down the road of apologies while on a guilt trip; rather, it's an extension of compassion and sensitivity toward a person whose life experiences do not line up with ours.

When I (D. A.) have been given the grace to speak publicly about systemic oppression and racism, I've found believers who share a similar narrative as mine overwhelmingly embrace my content. Yet, at the same time, there are those who implicitly reject it, who assume I embellished details of my story simply because they have never had similar encounters. Rather than getting upset, I've learned to take time to walk them through the reality of life for ethnic minorities who are indigenous to the oppressive struggle.

I've come to learn that expressing grief over poor educational systems, lack of good-paying jobs, affordable housing, and racial profiling are not always the best examples to lead with. I've learned to start my responses with a topic that transcends race and lends itself to every human: hunger. I ask them to list the grocery stores that are close to where they live. Often they're able to list at least a few major chain stores they frequent. After hearing them, I share with them the fact low-income communities of color have 50 percent fewer grocery stores within the radius of their neighborhoods than their higher income, predominately white counterparts[26] in low-income supermarkets; there is 20 percent less produce available; and what is available is 30 percent more expensive.[27]

In most cases, the conversation has become more empathetic at this point because we begin to see people not as numbers or colors initially, rather as human beings who are image bearers of God and have need for nourishment. From this point on, the one showing empathy now has a greater desire to hear about other forms of oppression, so they can be mobilized to minister to those who are suffering! Only the Lord can produce such heart change.

We've also learned to root our comments regarding national moments of racial conflict in Scripture, not our opinions. The morning after the Walter Scott killing video went viral, I (D. A.) was blessed to speak in chapel at Charleston Southern University. The campus is positioned six miles away from where Scott was killed in North Charleston. I felt impressed to exposit Matthew 5:38–42. During my message I encouraged all the students to be honest with their emotions during our conversations with believers of other ethnicities in regards to racial conflicts, yet always subject their emotions to the truth of God's Word.

After the sermon I was approached by a retired North Charleston police officer who is a close friend of the officer who shot Scott. He expressed thankfulness for the sermon being true to the words of Christ while showing my expression of empathy for the officer. I informed him I learned through interpersonal communication with police officers I've pastored to remember they are image bearers of God and put their lives on the line daily. This reality has caused me to affirm them in public while reminding ethnic minorities to pray for them as well. Once we allow ourselves to listen to the hearts of those we communicate with and humble ourselves to learn from them, we'll become more equipped to express sincere empathy and sympathy to others when it counts.

Live

In Scripture, living life together as "one another" was one countercultural distinction the body of Christ personified to the pagan world around them. As we continually listen and learn from each other, we'll gain great momentum within the body of Christ to keep on pursuing life together. By staying faithful to listening and learning, our love for the body of Christ will grow and mature.

We must turn to Scripture in order to calibrate our hearts with God's—guiding us in the common realities of human life as we share with those we live with who are different from us. We're all image bearers of God (Gen. 1:26–27), Eve is the mother of us all (Gen. 3:20), and we've all inherited a sin nature from our common father Adam (Rom. 5:12–21). Yet in spite of our sinfulness, for those of us who are in Christ, we're now new creatures

(2 Cor. 5:17) who make up the one new man (Eph. 2:14–16) Christ purchased with His blood. We're family!

Sharing our lives with family is not always going to come with ease. Because we are sinful human beings who are still being redeemed, there will be interpersonal conflicts that arise outside of conversations dealing with race. We all have personal preferences, lack communication skills, and have a lot of baggage from previous wounds in our lives. People who see the unveiled contents of our hearts are those we live with.

In Ephesians 4:1–3 Paul commands believers to walk in community in such a way that we're extending gentleness, patience, and accepting each other while keeping the unity of the Spirit with the peace that binds us. When we live life together as family during the moments of irritation, we're given opportunity to respond in gentleness (Prov. 15:1). When our brothers and sisters in Christ start getting on our nerves, we can rejoice in the fact God has provided us an opportunity to extend them patience (Col. 3:12–13).

Our culture needs to see what God's work looks like in the "present tense" lives of His saints. In 1 Thessalonians 2:8 Paul sets for us a model of how we are to do this. He informed the Thessalonians the reason he desired to be around them and share the gospel and himself with them was because they were dear to him. In essence, he loved them and saw living life with them as a blessing.

Imagine how our culture would react if they saw believers—believers from a diversity of cultures, ethnicities, genders, generations, and socioeconomic backgrounds—serving (Gal. 5:13), receiving (Rom. 15:7), being kind (Eph. 4:32), not judging (Rom. 14:13), and caring for and suffering with one another (1 Cor. 12:25–26). Our lifestyle would match the profession of our lips as it relates to racial reconciliation. We would render our culture with no excuse for not pursuing the God who reconciled us to Him and each other.

Conclusion

At this juncture, we would earn back the credibility to lead the conversation on racial reconciliation. We would be able to lead by walking our culture through truthful assessments of the church's poor gospel stewardship of the past only to juxtapose it with our example of reconciliation personified in our churches now. When they wander into our churches, they'd be greeted with a real-life brochure of heaven as read about in Revelation 7:9.

What sounds romantic should be the church's reality. Our nation has never been in a greater position to lead than ever before. Over 80 percent of our population lives in urban centers[28] where the nations inhabit our neighborhoods. America is browning[29] and the church must keep sharing the gospel message of Christ shedding His red blood for sinners of all hues.

With the business world already asking for wisdom on how they can adjust our nation's demographic shift,[30] what better example than for them to inquire of the church. It's as if God has put us in a position to show the world what unity amongst the nations looks like—demonstrating how to work through and resolve conflict through the employment of interpersonal communication and the application of Scripture.

Discussion Questions

1. In what ways does the church get to offer a better witness on race than what the culture offers?
2. How have you seen shortcomings in how the church has maybe copied some attitudes in the culture on race?
3. In what ways have you seen racism remain a factor in American life?

ADDITIONAL READING

United: Captured by God's Vision for Diversity by Trillia Newbell

Disunity: Uncovering the Hidden Forces that Keep Us Apart by Christena Cleveland

Letters to a Birmingham Jail: A Response to the Words and Dreams of Dr. Martin Luther King Jr. by Bryan Lorritts

Reviving the Black Church: New Life for a Sacred Institution by Thabiti Anyabwile

Bloodlines: Race, Cross, and the Christian by John Piper

Aliens in the Promised Land: Why Minority Leadership Is Overlooked in White Christian Churches and Institutions by Anthony Bradley

The Decline of African American Theology: From Biblical Faith to Cultural Captivity by Thabiti Anyabwile

Right Color, Wrong Culture: The Type of Leader Your Organization Needs to Become Multiethnic by Bryan Lorritts

Ethnic Blends: Mixing Diversity into Your Local Church by Mark Deymaz and Harry Li

ACKNOWLEDGMENTS

To the many hands inside and outside the ERLC, we thank you for your help and assistance on this book. The ERLC team provided joyful encouragement in the planning and execution of this series, and without them, it would never have gotten off the ground. We want to also personally thank Phillip Bethancourt who was a major visionary behind this project, along with our friends Andrew and Eric Wolgemuth. Last, the excellent team at B&H, led by Devin Maddox and Jennifer Lyell, provided the type of leadership and vision that channels creativity with a focus toward impacting local churches.

ABOUT THE ERLC

The ERLC is dedicated to engaging the culture with the gospel of Jesus Christ and speaking to issues in the public square for the protection of religious liberty and human flourishing. Our vision can be summed up in three words: kingdom, culture, and mission.

Since its inception, the ERLC has been defined around a holistic vision of the kingdom of God, leading the culture to change within the church itself and then as the church addresses the world. The ERLC has offices in Washington, DC, and Nashville, Tennessee.

ABOUT THE CONTRIBUTORS

Thabiti Anyabwile is a pastor at Anacostia River Church. He and his wife have three children. They live and minister in southeast Washington, DC.

Matthew J. Hall (Ph.D., University of Kentucky) is vice president of Academic Services at The Southern Baptist Theological Seminary, where he also teaches classes in church history.

J. Daniel Hays serves as dean of the Pruet School of Christian Studies at Ouachita Baptist University.

D. A. Horton currently serves as the teaching pastor at Reach Fellowship in South Los Angeles County.

Eric Mason is founder and lead pastor of Epiphany Fellowship in Philadelphia, Pennsylvania.

Trillia Newbell serves as director of Community Outreach for The Ethics and Religious Liberty Commission and is the author of *Fear and Faith* (2015) and *United* (2014).

NOTES

1. John R. W. Stott, *Human Rights and Human Wrongs: Major Issues for a New Century* (Grand Rapids, MI: Baker, 1999), 174–75.

2. For a more detailed discussion, see J. Daniel Hays, *From Every People and Nation: A Biblical Theology of Race*, NSBT (Downers Grove, IL: IVP, 2003), 52–54.

3. See the discussion on this marriage in Hays, *From Every People and Nation*, 70–77.

4. Craig S. Keener, *A Commentary on the Gospel of Matthew* (Grand Rapids, MI: Eerdmans, 1999), 79–80. See also Hays, *From Every People and Nation*, 158–60.

5. Richard Bauckham, *The Climax of Prophecy: Studies in the Book of Revelation* (Edinburgh: T & T Clark, 1993), 336. See also Hays, *From Every People and Nation*, 193–200.

6. Hays, *From Every People and Nation*, 201–6.

7. C. S. Lewis, *The Weight of Glory* (New York: HarperOne, 2001), 45–46.

8. Jarvis Williams, *One New Man: The Cross and Racial Reconciliation in Pauline Theology* (Nashville, B&H Academic, 2010), 88.

9. See http://www.people.com/article/jay-z-hip-hop-impacts-race.

10. W. Arndt, F. W. Danker, and W. Bauer, *A Greek-English Lexicon of the New Testament and Other Early Christian Literature*, 3rd ed. (Chicago: University of Chicago Press, 2000), 521.

11. W. A. Elwell and B. J. Beitzel, *Baker Encyclopedia of the Bible* (Grand Rapids, MI: Baker Book House, 1988), 1823–24.

12. J. L. Mays, ed. *Harper's Bible Commentary* (San Francisco, CA: Harper & Row, 1988), 804.

13. "PBS Probes Slave-Owning Issue; Affleck Expresses Regret," http://www.nytimes.com/aponline/2015/04/21/us/ap-us-sony-hack-wikileaks-affleck.html?_r=0.

14. Michael O. Emerson and Christian Smith, *Divided by Faith: Evangelical Religion and the Problem of Race in America* (New York: Oxford University Press, 2000), 7.

15. For more on the Southern Baptist Convention and race, see Paul Harvey, *Redeeming the South: Religious Cultures and Racial Identities Among Southern Baptists, 1865–1925* (Chapel Hill: University of North Carolina Press, 1997); Mark Newman, *Getting Right with God: Southern Baptists and Desegregation, 1945–1995* (Tuscaloosa: University of Alabama Press, 2001).

16. For more on the development of a theological worldview that constructed the idea of race and legitimized slavery, see Richard A. Bailey, *Race and Redemption in Puritan New England* (New York: Oxford University Press, 2011); Rebecca Anne Goetz, *The Baptism of Early Virginia: How Christianity Created Race* (Baltimore: Johns Hopkins University Press, 2012).

17. See, for example, Christopher Cameron, *To Plead Our Own Cause: African Americans in Massachusetts and the Making of the Antislavery Movement* (Kent, OH: Kent State University Press, 2014); Mark Noll, *The Civil War as a Theological Crisis* (Chapel Hill, NC: University of North Carolina Press, 2006).

18. See David L. Chappell, *A Stone of Hope: Prophetic Religion and the Death of Jim Crow* (Chapel Hill: University of North Carolina Press, 2005); Carolyn Renée Dupont, *Mississippi Praying: Southern White Evangelicals and the Civil Rights Movement, 1945–1975* (New York: New York University Press, 2013).

19. For more on the history of these biblical interpretations, see Fay Botham, *Almighty God Created the Races: Christianity, Interracial Marriage, and American Law* (Chapel Hill, NC: University of North Carolina Press, 2009), 93–111; Stephen R. Haynes, *Noah's Curse: The Biblical Justification of American Slavery* (New York: Oxford University Press, 2002).

20. John Leadley Dagg, *The Elements of Moral Science* (New York: Sheldon & Company, 1860), 344–45.

21. Charles Marsh and John M. Perkins, *Welcoming Justice: God's Movement Toward Beloved Community* (Downers Grove, IL: InterVarsity Press, 2010), 37.

22. Christopher Ingraham, "Three quarters of whites don't have any non-white friends," http://www.washingtonpost.com/blogs/wonkblog /wp/2014/08/25/three-quarters-of-whites-dont-have-any-non-white -friends, accessed May 1, 2015.

23. Gordon W. Allport, *The Nature of Prejudice: 25th Anniversary Edition* (New York: Perseus Books, 1979), 281.

24. Thomas F. Pettigrew, Linda R. Tropp, "A meta-analytic test of intergroup contact theory," *Journal of Personality and Social Psychology,* Vol 90 (5), May 2006: 751–83.

25. According to a 2013 American Values Survey (AVS), 75 percent of the white Americans polled said their social network of people they discuss important matters with are entirely white, with no minority presence. For black Americans, the number drops to 65 percent (of a completely black network), while 46 percent of Hispanics reported having a completely Hispanic network. Public Religion Research Institute, "Race and Americans' Social Networks," http://publicreligion .org/research/2014/08/analysis-social-network/#.VUNxx86lmCQ, accessed on May 1, 2015.

26. S. Treuhaft and A. Karpyn, "The Grocery Gap: Who Has Access to Healthy Food and Why It Matters," 2011, http://www.policy link.org/site/c.lkIXLbMNJrE/b.5860321/k.A5BD/The_Grocery_Gap .htm.

27. California Center for Public Health Advocacy, "Designed for disease: the link between local food environments and obesity and diabetes," 2008, Davis, CA. Retrieved from http://www.policylink.org/documents/DesignedforDisease.pdf.

28. "American Community Survey," http://proximityone.com/urbanpopulation.htm, accessed on May 1, 2015.

29. Sandra L. Colby and Jennifer M. Ortman, "Projections of the Size and Composition of the U.S. Population: 2014 to 2060," http://www.census.gov/content/dam/Census/library/publications/2015/demo/p25-1143.pdf, accessed on May 1, 2015.

30. Glenn Llopis, "Preparing U.S. Leadership for the Cultural Demographic Shift," http://www.forbes.com/sites/glennllopis/2014/07/21/preparing-u-s-leadership-for-the-cultural-demographic-shift, accessed on May 1, 2015.